Kate Waterman Hamilton

Rachel's Share of the Road

Kate Waterman Hamilton

Rachel's Share of the Road

ISBN/EAN: 9783744678476

Printed in Europe, USA, Canada, Australia, Japan

Cover: Foto ©Thomas Meinert / pixelio.de

More available books at **www.hansebooks.com**

ROUND-ROBIN SERIES

Rachel's Share of the Road

BOSTON

JAMES R. OSGOOD AND COMPANY

1882

CONTENTS.

Rachel's Share of the Road.

CHAPTER I.

HEADS HAVE IT.

FROM the east, along the narrow iron road
that cleft the hill and spanned the river,
rushed the morning train, and with clanging
bell, shrieking whistle and heavy, panting
breath, paused before an unpretending station.

"Craig's Cross!"

A very few passengers, gathering up wraps
and travelling-bags, left the cars; others
looked half curiously, half indifferently, from
the windows for a moment, and discovering
no object of special interest, leaned wearily

back in their seats again. But a fragment of
the town was visible, and even if fully seen
it would not have attracted much attention —
a small place whose chief importance centred
in the great railroad shops clustered there.

On the long platform fronting the depot
were gathered the usual little knots of loun-
gers who watched the train with idle interest,
while, scattered here and there, were some
who scanned its line of windows with anxious
faces — disappointed faces — as it thundered
away on its course once more.   Apart from all
others, at a little distance from the depot itself,
and hidden from the observation of the group
on the platform, stood a heavy, shabbily
dressed figure with one coarse hand resting on
the head of an equally heavy and shabby dog.
Not near enough to distinguish any one who
entered or left the carriages, yet the hungry
eyes under the old hat never swerved for an
instant from their steadfast watching until the
last trail of smoke from the receding engine

had vanished. Then the man turned, not toward the town, but away from it, along a road winding up the hill, until, reaching a tree that extended its branches over the sunny, dusty grass, he threw himself down beneath its shade.

"Clingo, you don't know no more nor I do."

The dog acknowledged his name by a slight motion of his tail, but looked gravely down the road without asserting any claim to superior wisdom.

The master pushed his hat back from his face — a young face only negatively; it was not old in years, but there was no youthfulness about it — rough, sunburned, heavy. He drew his sleeve across his damp forehead, and turned his eyes — not unlike the dog's in a certain dumb wistfulness — toward tree, cloud and wayside as if seeking counsel.

"Don't know if he's come; s'pose 'taint no use noway," he muttered, plucking at a long withe of grass with an odd nervousness in the great, hard, red hand that was only strong, not quick nor skilful. " 'Taint likely he'd listen. Don't know whether I'll say nothin' if I see him a-comin'. Wonder if "—

The sentence was left unfinished in a slowly dawning suggestion. He drew a solitary copper from his pocket and poised it on one broad finger.

" We'll toss up for't, Clingo. Heads, we tries it; tails, we don't."

The coin went spinning into the air, and dropped at his feet. Clingo arose and solemnly sniffed at it; then his master examined it.

" Heads — wonst! "

Again the bit of copper whirled and fell.

" Heads — twicet! "

" Heads — three times. Heads has it." And returning the cent to its place, he leaned back against the tree and waited.

Up on the hill, in a great pleasant old house lying in roomy, solid comfort behind its old-fashioned garden of terraces and quaint arbors of clambering roses and nodding tiger-lilies, another also waited. All the view down the slope and away to the distant hills and river was loveliness in the bright morning light, but the gray eyes at the window for once looked straight through the beauty as scarcely seeing it, and watched only for a carriage on the winding road. A tiny clock in the spacious room told the minutes, lessening one by one the number of those that held any expectation in them, and Rachel, noting their flight, sighed a little anxiously, but more wearily.

"He isn't coming this morning!"

Doubtless the same thought, concerning the same individual, found expression in many different voices, with various intonations of sorrow, vexation or disappointment, as that morning hour passed; for Judge Lyndal, president of the road, was invariably wanted at one end of the line when he was at the other. It had often amused Rachel — the stream of inquiries made for him in his frequent absences. Anxious contractors, eager place-seekers, perplexed office-men, all wanting to know when the Judge would come home. "As if he were like the sun, and nothing were left for one half the world but waiting and darkness when he visited the other half," she laughingly said.

She remembered them this morning, finding herself among the waiting ones — though her disappointment involved only the postponement of a pleasant trip, planned chiefly for the sake of the cousins who were to accompany her. They had wished to start that morning, but Rachel could not well go until her father returned. All the previous day they had expected him, and he had not arrived yet. It was very annoying — not that she cared so much for the excursion beyond the feeling, scarcely admitted to her own consciousness, that jaunting with Nan and Heman might be a little less tiresome than staying at home with

them. After the first week their visiting together always grew somewhat laborious.

Perhaps it was only Rachel who found it so
— " an odd, old-fashioned little thing, suiting
exactly the old house and grounds," Nan said
of her, so disposing, with calm superiority, of
all points in their intercourse where the want
of congeniality revealed itself. And of these
Nan did not detect many. She had no quick
ear for spiritual harmonies, and seldom noticed
the subtile jarrings and discords that so perplexed and wearied Rachel. In truth, Nan
was always too deeply absorbed in the rendi-
tion of her own little part to ever catch life's
music as a whole. So she liked well enough
the regular half-yearly visits to her cousin and
the old place, — thought them the proper
thing for certain seasons of the year, — though
she felt a pitying condemnation of Rachel as
a wonder of wasted opportunities. With her
father's position and wealth, what place and
influence might not be hers if she did but

appreciate her advantages. "It is a positive duty to make the most of what one has," said Nan — a favorite axiom, repeated quite as impressively when she discussed the remodelling of a gown as when she spoke of a life.

"Only there is always the question of what is 'the most,'" Rachel answered, with that sudden deepening of her gray eyes that Annice Lisle could not understand.

A twofold life, a twofold personality, her own sometimes seemed to the young girl, in which "most" or best was not always clearly discernible. In the city, with her father's friends, she had been, or seemed to herself, only a gay young girl, as gloriously apparelled as the lilies, and far more useless than they, perhaps, but content to enjoy her surroundings, and a certain reflected honor and importance. She had thought and talked, with a little harmless, girlish complacency, of "our road." It had meant to her only a high position of responsibility and honor for her

father, — deserved, of course, — gay parties
made up for trial trips with new engines and
palace cars, and a pleasant sense of proprietorship in it all; unbounded courtesy and attention to herself whenever she chose to travel up
or down the line.

But here, in the still, grand old home, a
deeper meaning seemed to underlie many
things. Do souls grow, like their natural surroundings? Almost it seemed as if into
Rachel's, something of the strength and brave
upreaching of the hills were passing; something of the steady onward sweep of the river
looking out from her eyes. Here, in the
quiet of hills and river, the narrow iron road,
stretching so endlessly away, wore a harder,
sterner aspect, and held strange suggestions,
sometimes, of those to whom it represented a
dreary and toilsome life-track — the weary
men who laid rail and tie, the anxious men to
whom a place on the swift-rushing trains that
passed and repassed meant the earning of a

livelihood for themselves and their dear ones; and the rude cabins by the roadside, where the poor workmen found a shelter when the day's pittance was earned.

Rachel knew of all these. Some strange acquaintances Judge Lyndal's daughter had made in the long, unquestioned rambles permitted to her lonely, motherless childhood. She had known of them without thinking much, however, until of late; but there was ample space and leisure for thought in that quiet, roomy house on the hillside, where even the vines swayed dreamily, and the rustling leaves whispered of secrets long kept; where the life seemed to have grown even stiller and more uneventful than of old, from its contrast with the city months.

The sedate old walls entertained but little company. Rachel's stately, invalid grandmother, the nominal mistress of the place, had neither inclination nor strength for society; and her wish for seclusion, together with the

Judge's frequent absences, would have rendered the gathering of any large circle about
her there impracticable to Rachel, if she had
wished it. But, accustomed to the existing
order as she had been from her childhood,
she did not even think of having it otherwise.
So she saw few but passing guests — grave,
business-like men who talked with her father
of "bonds," "stocks" and "dividends" — save
when Nan and Heman came. Their visits
had occurred simultaneously the last two or
three seasons.

"I am very sorry we are disappointed," said
the young hostess, the pressure of entertaining
the two arousing her from the reverie into
which she was falling while her eyes scanned
the road. "He could not have been on this
morning's train. I fear we must wait another
day."

"Well, if we cannot do what we expected,
we must try to plan something else equally
pleasant — and profitable," responded Heman,

with cheerful resignation in his carefully modulated tones, but with an air of being all ready to have something planned for him instead. "These bright hours are far too valuable to be wasted in mere regret."

Rachel felt a mischievous inclination to inquire from which of his six sermons written, or six hundred yet to be written, he had extracted that edifying platitude; but, discovering Nan's glance of admiring appreciation, she restrained the impulse. Their cousinly relation to Rachel did not extend to each other, but there was manifest, in these later visits, a stronger bond between them than that of kinship.

The sun that smiled upon the nodding lilies and sleepy poppies of the garden that morning beat hot and bright upon the dry and dusty road with its border of soiled and tired-looking daisies, and an old woman who was making the ascent with resolute step assured herself audibly now and then:

"It's proper warm, I tell ye!"

Her dress of faded calico was short and
scant, while her antiquated black bonnet,
pushed far enough back from her heated face
to show a rim of rough gray hair, was the
worse for many a bruise and dent. One
hand, purple as berry stains could make it,
grasped the handle of her gray cotton parasol,
while the other carried a large basket of fruit
covered carefully with green leaves. As she
neared the great tree by the roadside a voice
stopped her:

"Say, do you know if the Judge has got
home?"

"No, I don't. If ye want anything of him
it's more'n likely he hain't," answered the old
woman, putting down her basket and turning
squarely about to view her questioner. "Do
ye know what that man makes me think of?
— a spider. 'Cause all these railroad lines is
stretched here and there like a great web, and
folks twisted into 'em and wrigglin' about, one

way or 'nother; but when ye want to find the
big bug that spins 'em all, why, he's hid away
out of sight — weavin' and weavin' somewheres, I'll warrant!"

The man under the tree did not appear to
comprehend; he only looked up dully, and
the old woman took her basket again.

"Well, I'm going right there, and I can ask
whether he's come, if it'll be any sort of comfort to ye," she said.

A touch of eagerness betrayed itself in the
heavy face then.

"Yes'm.   Wish you would."

The woman trudged on again.   Reaching
the garden gate she turned aside and walked
up the gravelled path, with never a glance for
the flowers, across the veranda, and, catching
sight of the form at the window, straight into
the cool, shadowy room where Rachel sat.
There, dropping into an easy chair, she
deposited her basket beside her, pushed her

battered bonnet a little farther back, and began rocking vigorously to and fro.

"Good morning, Mrs. Shackles," said Rachel, undismayed, while Nan looked dignified but undisguised disapproval.

"Mornin', child, — dear knows about the good! All out doors is a-blisterin' and a-br'il-in', and here you set lookin' as calm and comfor'able as a pond-lily with nothin' but its head out of water. It does 'pear 's if some folks was jest made to set and look aggravatin' in shaddery places, while other folks travels by in the glare and dust. Want to buy any huckleberries? Only five cents a quart, and I picked 'em fresh this mornin' —up afore daybreak."

She of the sheltered, shady nook had a tender spot in her heart for those of the rough highway. Moreover, this was an old acquaintance — one of the odd delights of her childhood. The stained, scratched hands and the gray hair held in them a mighty appeal to her; so she wanted "huckleberries" now, just as she had wanted raspberries earlier, and would be sure to want sassafras later. They were sent out to the kitchen, measured and paid for, but the old woman sat still, resting and moralizing, while her wandering eyes scanned every article in the room, not excepting, nor abashed by, the gentleman and lady who were strangers to her.

"Yes'm, huckleberries and milk is partic'lar good — 'specially if ye has the milk; some folks hain't. That's what I tell Humphrey when he says why don't we have bread and milk and huckleberries, seein' I'm pickin' so many of 'em. He's al'ays sayin', 'Ask somebody for't;' but I ain't no hand at beggin'. Ho! hum! Mebby I'd get along better if I was."

"Oh, I think Peggy can give you a pail of milk if you would like it," said Rachel cheerily.

"Dear! now that's proper good; but la! I

hain't got no pail to put it in. I've been
wishin' I had one this long time, 'cause 'twould
come so handy; and Humphrey says, ' Why
don't you ask some of them folks what's got
more'n they want?' But I tells him, ' Humphrey Shackles, I never did beg afore I
married ye, and I ain't a-goin' to begin now,
if I work my fingers off.' So I hain't got no
pail, and no prospeck of gettin' none.'

"No matter; I'll ask Peggy to put the milk
in one that you needn't return," laughed
Rachel.

"Thank ye; that'll be a comfort — jest will.
Must be nice to have plenty so's you can give
away to the poor and deservin', ain't it now?
That's what I told Mrs. Reeves 'tother day,
when she give me a wash-tub; though sakes!
'twant no use 'thout a wash-board, and she
never seemed to think of that. 'Course I
couldn't ask her, 'cause I don't b'lieve in beggin', and so it lays 'round."

Rachel tried to keep the sparkle of fun from

her eyes, while she wondered what was next on the list; but Heman Weldon could no longer restrain the mild exhortation which he thought the occasion demanded.

"My cousin follows only her own kindly impulses in this quiet place; but she would soon discover such encouragement to be not beneficial, but positively injurious, if she had a parish on her hands," he said, with a significant, reproving glance as he passed from the room.

He had not expected Mrs. Shackles to comprehend the remark, but she gleaned something of his meaning, and her sharp eyes followed him.

"What does the young man expect to have on his hands?" she questioned. "Nothin' but what he can wash off easy, by the looks of 'em."

Rachel bit her lips.

"He was talking of city work. My cousin intends to be a minister. Mrs. Shackles."

"Preacher? Oh, well, there's some kinds of preachers — and then there's other kinds," said the old woman, not quite satisfied. "Dear me, some preach one thing, and some another."

"But truth is always truth. Heman will preach that " — Rachel began the latter sentence to herself rather than to either of her auditors, and, recollecting them, suddenly paused.

"Yes, truth's always truth. Same way apples is always apples, but the dried ones ain't very satisfyin' to most folks, nor partic'lar wholesome either, as I know of," responded Mrs. Shackles, nodding her head by way of emphasis. Then her eyes wandered around the room again, rested meditatively on a bracket, and she took up her former line of remark.

"Yes, there's lots of things I need — frocks and shoes and sich. But nobody don't know about it, and never will by my tellin', so I s'pose I shan't get none."

Rachel had grown suddenly obtuse, and inquired after Humphrey — where he was, and what he was doing.

"Outside somewheres : down at the foot of the hill, a-hangin' round and waitin'; and I can't tell ye what for, 'cause I don't know. He come along a-ways to-day, and I give him the basket to fetch, seein' I'd been out so long a-pickin'. But he didn't carry it no time afore it give him the cramp in his left hand, and d'rectly it brought a touch of rheumatiz to his right hand, and pretty soon he set down. 'And now I s'pose you've got the dumb ager in both feet?' says I; and he 'lowed mebby he had. So I come on; and it's likely he's settin' there yet. If there ever was a body good for nothin' it's Humphrey Shackles. He spunks up now and then when I tell him so, and says he'll do somethin' desp'ate yet, when he gets screwed up to the stickin' p'int. And I says, 'Humphrey Shackles, you'll never get screwed to that p'int while there's a breath of life in ye ' — and no more he won't. Well, I must be goin'. I'm 'bliged to ye for the pail and wash-board."

"Milk," corrected Rachel.

"Oh, yes, milk. I'm real glad you thought on't. I don't mind takin' things when anybody gives 'em; but I won't beg, so I s'pose I'll never get no shoes and gowns and sich, bad as I need 'em, 'cause, you see, nobody don't know."

She drew her old bonnet further over her head, while her eyes sought Rachel's face with a curious sidelong glance to mark the effect of this last carefully aimed hint. It seemed to have glanced off harmlessly, and she took up her basket with a sigh. Then, with a sudden thought of the stranger under the tree, she turned again.

"S'pose the Judge ain't home now?"

"No," Rachel answered. "We expected him, but he did not come."

Which information Mrs. Shackles repeated

when she had passed half way down the road.

" They looked for him and he didn't come. Everybody's al'ays lookin' for him when he don't come. It's what he's made for, likely. But see here, if you want anything of him you might as well ask her," indicating by a backward motion of one stained hand the house she had left.

"Her?" echoed the man uncomprehendingly.

"His darter. I ain't any hand at beggin' myself, but if I wanted anything I'd ask her," explained Mrs. Shackles.

"I ain't a beggar!" A flash of anger kindled the heavy eyes for an instant. "It's only work I want. The folks has got to live —Hitty and the children. I promised Meg I'd take care of the children; but it's been tough work. I thought I could get something in the shops here, but one says one thing, and another says another; and there's so many, and I hain't got no recommend from nobody. The Judge, he seems the topmost, and I thought mebby if I could ask the powerfullest" — said the unconscious St. Christoper slowly rising.

"Might as well ask her," interposed Mrs. Shackles.

"Mebby. Don't know if it's any use noways; but we're bound to try 'count of the luck turnin' so, hey, Clingo? Heads has it."

" 'Course. Heads al'ays has it," muttered Mrs. Shackles uncomprehendingly. "But me and you ain't heads, nor never will be, unless it's in that queer time comin' we're told about, when the last'll be first." And with a final hitch to her basket she went on down the road to meet Humphrey, while the man and dog began slowly to ascend by the way she had come.

CHAPTER II.

A DAY LOANED.

MY dear child!" expostulated Annice Lisle as the old berry-woman disappeared from the veranda. Nan was two years older and two inches taller than her cousin, which prove conclusively her superior wisdom and experience, and enabled her always to feel that she spoke from a slight eminence. "How absurd of you to indulge such a character as that! and to tolerate her manner, which was almost — excuse me, my dear — *neighborly*."

Rachel laughed. Under the laugh arose an old question — "Who is my neighbor?" But she did not utter it. Nan would have considered it either irrelevant or irreverent. A step on the stair interrupted them. Dr.

Kelsey was coming down from a call upon old Mrs. Lyndal. A venerable, gray-haired physician, the oldest in the place, attended her usually; Dr. Kelsey only occasionally, when his senior was ill or absent. He bowed to both ladies, though he seemed to see only Rachel, as he passed through the wide hall. On the veranda, his gaze swept the garden; he paused and glanced again toward the open window.

"Miss Lyndal, if you cared to send some of those blossoms on a mission this morning, I am going where they would be prized — where such things are rare."

"Surely! I am glad you told me," was the swift reply. She hastened to the door, then paused.

"Nan, will you come?"

A subtile hope, whose springs she did not analyze, that Miss Lisle might deem the sun-shiny garden too warm, was disappointed. Nan, indeed, never grew warm and flushed and hurried as Rachel did, and when, in a moment, she appeared on the walk she was cool, calm elegance personified.

"If you are at leisure?"—began Dr. Kelsey, as if in half apology for his request.

"Only too much so," laughed Rachel. "A plan disappointed this morning has left me a day, and I do not know what to do with it."

"What a pity you cannot lend it! So many hurried, crowded lives need a little extra time," the doctor answered.

Possibly he was thinking of his own as one of them, for he made no politely sympathetic inquiries concerning her frustrated plans—did not seem to think of them, indeed, but to feel only a covetous, momentary desire to appropriate the spare hours. He caught her glance and smiled at his own earnestness.

"We have so often to prescribe time as a remedy that it is not wonderful I begin to think of it as a marketable article."

"Not exactly as a 'drug in the market,'

however?" questioned Nan lightly, a trifle condescendingly to this "country doctor," as she mentally styled him.

He did not appear impressed by her graciousness, however, answering only by a quiet smile, as if the remark naturally called for nothing more, and bestowing his full attention upon the flowers Rachel was selecting — cutting swiftly and dexterously the stems she touched — his hand, white and well-shaped, but large, strong and steady, contrasting oddly with her slender, fluttering fingers. Something in his face, manly and strong rather than handsome, — a certain searching earnestness in the clear eyes, as if they had a fashion of looking through externals straight to the heart of things, — interested while it piqued Nan. She became doubly gracious, and bestowed upon him, for a little time, her most delicate flattery of attention and entertaining remark.

But though he listened appreciatively, evidently enjoying the hour, the view from the hillside, and his companionship, he did not linger. And when, seeing his glance follow for an instant the sweep of hill and river, she asked his opinion — a question in which a little malice mingled with some vanity — of the relative beauty of this scenery and various views in foreign lands, he answered with quiet honesty, —

"I cannot tell, Miss Lisle. I have seen much of our own country in a sort of rough knocking about, scarcely to be dignified as travelling, but I have never been abroad; probably shall never have that pleasure until I have attained old age, wealth and uselessness at home," concluding his sentence with a laugh, not unabashed by, but simply unconscious of, the superiority of the presence in which he stood.

The flowers gathered, he took his leave hastily, and mounted the horse awaiting him at the gate, pausing a moment, however, to

select a choice rose-bud from his treasures and
fasten it in his button-hole.

"Cool!" commented Nan, observing the
movement.

Rachel flushed, and answered with a slight
embarrassed laugh, —

"A precautionary measure for his health,
perhaps; roses may be disinfectants. Merely
professional, — like his steady way of looking
at one."

"Looking at *one* is a very correct way of
stating it. He certainly did not look at more
than one," replied Nan loftily, turning toward
the house.

Rachel loitered a little, watching the swiftly
receding horseman, and so became conscious,
a moment later, of a figure outside the wall.
A head surmounted by a dilapidated hat appeared above the gate, and its owner called,
rather hesitatingly and huskily, —

"Marm! If you please, marm!"

Rachel advanced a few steps, but stopped

in alarm as a pair of shaggy paws were placed on the rail, and a huge canine head also appeared above the gate.

"He won't bite, marm. Down, Clingo, down!"

"Do you wish to see any one? What is wanted?" inquired Rachel, questioning mentally whether the intruder were tramp or beggar, or might possibly have a legitimate business errand.

"If I could speak to you a minute, marm — I s'pose the Judge ain't home?"

"No," she replied, going a little nearer. Those words, in one form or another, were so familiar, and the voice, despite its roughness, had a touch of entreaty. "He is not at home. Probably he will come this evening, though I could not promise it positively."

"I don't know whether it's any use if he was — s'pose mebby 'tain't; but then the luck turned so, and I'm in powerful need of work" —

"Work?" repeated the young lady, catching through that word a clue to his meaning. "You want work, then?"

"Work in the railroad shops or yards, or anywheres, marm. I don't s'pose the Judge 'tends to that sort of thing himself, and mebby 'twasn't no use to come; but there's so many, and one says one thing, and another says another, — that 'tain't no use to go to this place till I've been t'other place, and no use to ask this one till I've seen that one, — till I'm clean mixed up. And then there's so many want places. Sometimes it seems 's if this world had got crowded so chock full there wasn't no room for a feller noways."

A slight breeze swept through the garden, rustling the leaves and bending the blossoms, and the man at the gate bared his head to the cool, refreshing breath, revealing a shock of light hair burned and faded by the sun and wind, while he nervously twisted the old hat in his fingers.

"I hain't got no recommend — don't know nobody here, you see. Most folks sort o' belong to somebody, and that keeps 'em along; but I don't seem to, and I get most tired tryin'. I heard 'em sayin' round the shops — 'If the Judge gets back,' and 'When the Judge comes home;' and so thinks I he's the powerfullest of all of 'em, and if he'd say the word, — but I don't s'pose 'twas any use to ask."

However it might have been with the Judge, the Judge's daughter grew interested. She felt the sharp contrast between herself and this petitioner outside the gate, and the dumb appealing in the eyes of man and dog touched her.

"From where did you come?" she asked.

"Over the river, way back in the country, here a spell, and there a spell, harvestin', wood-choppin' or anything. But it got so there wasn't much of any kind to do round them parts; and the folks has got to live. I

promised Meg I'd take care of the children.
So we travelled across country, stoppin' between whiles this place and that as I'd get
odd jobs."

"You have children, then?"

"Marm? the twins? They was Meg's.
Bill, that's her husband, he'd hired a little
place, and I helped him work it some. But
he got killed, and Meg, that's my sister, you
see, she wasn't strong and well noways, and
she jest got thinner and whiter till she looked
like moonshine afore she died. And I'd hear
her a-cryin' and prayin' at nights — 'Oh, my
poor babies! they've got nobody — nobody!'
I couldn't stand it, so I took 'em, one on one
arm and t'other on t'other, and says I, 'Look
here, Meg, I'll take care of 'em. I ain't like
some for gettin' along, but I'll do my level
best, I will,' says I. Then she seemed more
satisfied like, but she didn't live only a day or
two. So I've done as good as I could, but it's
been sort of rough, with work hard to get,

and so many of us, — Hitty and the children and old Daddy. Do you s'pose, marm," — a sudden inspiration illuminating the dull brain, — "that the Judge'd take to me any more 'count of them twins? 'Cause I could bring 'em. Hitty'd fix 'em up. She's a master hand at patchin', if she is little."

The thought of such a presentation to her father — that man of stocks and bonds! — and its probable results, flashed a faint smile over Rachel's lips, but there was a deeper feeling in her eyes as she answered, —

"No, you need not do that. I will speak to my father for you if you wish. You have not told me your name?"

"Joe Baines, marm."

"I will tell him of you. I cannot promise anything. I do not know that he will think he can do anything in the matter of furnishing work for you," — pausing with a painful uncertainty in regard to the extent of her influence, — "but I will ask him."

But Joe entertained no doubt of her ability or success. If this young lady, the Judge's own daughter, spoke one word for him, his place must be sure. At last he had a friend at court. And he walked with quickened, lightened step as he retraced his way along the winding road.

Rachel, walking slowly back to the house, heard, through the open windows, the music of the piano — little tinkling sprays and jets of melody interspersed with bits of talk — as Nan's skilful fingers strayed over the keys in the pauses of her conversation with Heman. Finding them happily engaged, Rachel lingered for a few minutes in the hall, looking out with shadowed, thoughtful eyes on the picture the doorway framed. It was only a few minutes. A door opened far enough to admit the head of Peggy — a privileged personage, who was "Mrs. Larrison" to all the household, except her own especial pet and nursling.

"Somebody down stairs wants to know about the Judge. Of course there'll be a whole string of them now!" she said in her quick, short style. "You've nothing particular to tell them, Miss Rachel?"

"No."

Then something — the scene at the gate, or, perhaps, those earlier words about lending her spare day to other lives — awoke a sudden resolve to answer the inquiries herself this day. She remembered remorsefully how troubled and anxious were the faces that sometimes presented themselves there.

"I can tell them what little I do know; it may prove some satisfaction. I wish, while I am waiting, I could help some of the others to wait," she said, with a deepening feeling of sympathy for the disappointed ones.

A young Irishman looked up with pleasant, though not altogether cheerful, face as she entered the room.

"It's wantin' to ax about the Judge I was —

beg parding for disturbin' ye, miss. He didn't come home the day?"

"No," said Rachel. "We expected him, but he has not come."

"An' ye can't tell would he be in on the evenin' thrain?"

"No," she answered again. "I really don't know anything about it; I wish I did. We looked for him yesterday, and again this morning; but some business has detained him, I suppose, and I cannot tell when he will come."

The stranger's face fell; he studied the toe of his boot for a minute or two in silence.

"I am sorry," said Rachel.

He looked up then, half laughing, though not very cheerily.

"An' I'm that same, too, though it's mesilf couldn't be sayin' it would do much good if he was here. Ye see the paymaster's not been 'round the long while, an' I'm bothered wid hearin' one thing an' another about his comin':

so, as I was in town the day, — I works out on the road, — I thought I'd jist make bould to ax his honor himsilf could he tell me. If it would come in a day or two jist, sure I'd wait — though it's hard waitin'; but, seein' all the onsartainty, I'm thinkin' I'd bether go to Misther Corry an' be done wid it."

"Why, yes, I presume he could tell you as much about it as any one, — quite as much as my father," said innocent Rachel, pleased at the suggestion.

The man laughed again, not so pleasantly.

"Faith, that's the last place I'd be goin' for information, thin! It's to sell my time, I mane."

"Your time?" repeated the young lady, a little bewildered. "I don't understand. I thought you had sold your time already, — that is, that you were working for the railroad company, and they pay you for it."

"So they does, ma'am, — or they promises to, which isn't always the same thing — axin' yer parding"—suddenly remembering to whom he was speaking. "Ye see the pay is long comin' sometimes, an' when the childer get out of clothes an' the shanty out of pertaties, so the men can't do no longer, why, some of 'em sells their time — the bosses' 'count of the days they've worked, that is — to Misther Corry."

"Oh, I see! He advances the money, and receives it afterwards himself from the company? That is kind — though, of course, it doesn't cost him anything," — the last added reflectively.

"Not a bit of expinse to him, ma'am," responded the man grimly. "There's the triflin' difference that he makes a good dale by it, seein' he buys the time for fifty cints on the dollar."

Rachel started. She had been standing carelessly by a window, but she turned sharply about and looked the speaker steadily in the face.

"Do you mean to tell me that when the workmen need the money they have earned, Mr. Corry, an officer of the road, will buy it of them at only half what it is worth — half what has been promised them — and afterwards obtain for himself the whole amount from the company?" she questioned slowly.

"That's the way of it, ma'am."

"Then he does a cruel, dishonest, contemptible thing!" she exclaimed, her gray eyes flashing — quite forgetting the dignity of "our road," and speaking not at all like the politic President's daughter. "Takes advantage of their necessity, and uses their poverty to increase his own riches!"

The stranger's face lighted for a moment at her utter, vehement condemnation, as if he found some comfort in it, albeit only the poor one of hearing another say what he felt, but scarcely dared utter himself.

"It's like there's more than one thinks that, ma'am, only there's no good of their sayin' it.

But sometimes when they passes the fine house
he's buildin', they shakes their fists, but more
of 'em laughs an' says, 'I owns that fine win-
dy,' 'I paid for that illegant verandy.' Well,"
with an unsuccessful attempt at jocularity, "I
must be goin' to conthribute him another chim-
ney or sich-like."

Rachel watched him with absent, thoughtful
eyes as he turned to go. "I wonder," she said
rather uncertainly, "I wonder how it would do
for me to buy your time?"

The good-natured Irish face brightened —
sharpened somewhat, in truth — at thought of
making a better bargain with the lady than
would be possible with Mr. Corry.

"An' why shouldn't ye, ma'am, if ye like?"

"I scarcely know whether I can or not,"
Rachel proceeded still more hesitatingly. She
was as ignorant upon all business matters as
the most devout believer in woman's disabilities
and inabilities could desire. "Will you let me
see the account?"

They went over it together, he pointing awkwardly, now and then, to some item that needed explanation, while her slender white fingers turned the paper.

" Ye see ye'll get the whole of it from the company again."

" Yes, I think I shall," she answered, smiling faintly at thought of how unlikely it was that any one would offer her less than its full value, even if she wished it now; so far she had no doubt of her influence. But it was a sad smile, for why should this paper have more power in her hand than in that of this poor workman, except that his need was greater!

" So it's a nice little profit ye can be makin'," suggested the man, waiting with illy concealed eagerness for her offer of terms.

" Profit!" She recoiled as if a live coal had been offered for her grasping. " I do not deal in such profit as that. It may be considered a very shrewd way of buying time, but I should deem it a miserably poor way of selling more precious things."

Her words were more for herself than for her listener; but the quick, uneducated brain, the warm Irish heart, partly comprehended, and the look that flitted over his face told as much.

" I will take this, dollar for dollar," Rachel said, laying her hand on the paper. " Forty-one dollars and a half, isn't it? "

Silently, beyond a single very quiet " I'm sure I thank ye, ma'am," the man received the money. The voluble thanks and blessings usually so ready on a Celtic tongue did not come, but Rachel was satisfied that he was neither insensible nor ungrateful. She spurned that thought with some self-scorn, however, when the door had closed behind him.

" Grateful! why should he be for receiving only what he has earned? A mere act of justice, and one that cost me nothing."

She paced the long room once or twice, a hot flush on her young cheek, an indignant throbbing at her heart. This was not at all what "our road" had meant to her in the city. The deeper meaning that had only been coming to her of late, mere murmurings and suggestions, were growing into audible voices now.

Others came and went that day, and she saw them. The morning's fancy of putting her spare day into other lives clung to her, but more than that, she was awaking to a new strong interest.

At last, when the long hot day had burned itself into twilight and coolness, the Judge came home. Rachel waited still until, the evening far spent, and the claims of those two rivals, letters and newspapers, satisfied, the Judge leaned back in his chair for a little space with eyes wandering away to the golden stars, though in truth he was thinking of gold more marketable. Then she stole to a seat at his side, and told him something of her day and its revelations. Half smilingly, half absently, he listened, all the more smilingly because absently, perhaps.

"Sorry for your disappointment, my dear.
However, another day will do for your trip, I
suppose."

"Oh, yes! that is nothing. But, father,
about that other?"

"Other? Oh, your speculation in time, do
you mean? That will be made right, of
course; but I fear your tender-heartedness
will cost you much annoyance. Your Paddy
will undoubtedly tell how well he fared, and
you may be tormented by callers and importu-
nities without number. I wouldn't advise you
to repeat that bit of benevolence."

"But that wrong, father — the men having
to submit to such injustice because they cannot wait so long for their money? Cannot
that be helped? I thought you could do it."

"I? My dear child!" There was a blending of pity, amusement and impatience in his
tone. "Do you think I am the whole railroad
company? I find it quite enough to attend to
my own duties without shouldering those of

all the rest. As for the irregular pay-days —
why, a railroad isn't exactly like a pony-chaise
in the matter of expense, and certainly not in
the management required to run it. I suspect
Corry does drive sharp bargains with the
workmen sometimes — it is like him; but they
know it, and they should keep out of his
clutches. They are a thriftless, improvident
set, for the most part, who do not know how
to take care of what they get."

There was a moment's silence in which he
bestowed upon her unsatisfied, troubled face
a longer scrutiny than he usually gave it.

"You cannot understand it all, and there is
no use in worrying yourself over things that
you cannot help — nor I either," he said.
"About that fellow who asked for work —
Lane did you call him? — Blaine?"

"Baines."

"I have nothing to do with that; they
employ whom they will at the shops and yards,
of course. Still I do not mind speaking to

some of them to give him a chance if they have room for him and it will be any great satisfaction to you. It is doubtful whether he proves worth much, however. But really, Rachel, as I said before, I am not the whole company; and you must not attempt to satisfy all the people who come with all sorts of wants and stories, or you will have your hands more than full, and mine too."

She thanked him gravely for his promise regarding Joe, and the conference ended — the talk that Rachel had planned for all the day, that it should be a long, quiet talk, in which she and this busy father of hers should grow better acquainted than they had ever been before; for she remembered, with a sudden wondering, that she had never bestowed any confidences upon her father, that he had never sought them. But the conversation was ended.

CHAPTER III.

INTERWEAVING THREADS.

A DAY lent to other lives is unlike common loans in that it cannot be returned and become wholly one's own again. It is like the lending of threads to a swift-moving loom : they cannot be separated again, but must run on, twining and interweaving with all the others that make up the fabric. The delayed excursion was undertaken the next morning, — a bright beautiful morning, fair as that of the previous day. It was only Rachel who was not quite the same, who had grown somewhat wiser, perhaps a little sadder, since yesterday's pondering of vexed problems. But it was a difference felt only by herself, and not apparent to other eyes, certainly not to those of Mr. Stephen Corry, who was leisurely enjoying a cigar while he paced the length of the platform in front of the station and waited for the train. His face, a clearly cut, handsome face, brightened as he saw the party. He tossed the lighted cigar away, and joined them with evident pleasure in his greeting.

"I heard you were at home, Miss Lyndal, but I did not know that your cousins were here also. Are you going to inspect that famous new tunnel of ours out on the Western Branch? Fortunately for myself, I am bound upon the same errand."

"Not that our judgment upon the construction of tunnels is particularly valuable," Annice explained.

"Nor mine," he laughed.

> "'A tunnel through the hillside grim,
> A gloomy tunnel is to him,
> And it is nothing more,'—

Except as it is made so by pleasant company. But my father considers this one a triumph of engineering skill, — it is our road, you know,

—and as I have already been at home a week
it is my duty to visit it.   And virtue is its own
reward in this case," with another quick glance
at Rachel.   "There is our train.   Allow me,
Miss Rachel."   And he hastily gathered
shawl and veil from the carriage cushions and
threw them over his arm.

This easy familiarity was natural enough.
They had met often in the city.   Mr. Corry
had been a frequent visitor at her uncle's house,
joining the family pleasure-parties, and accompanying Rachel to concert and drive with a
sort of friendly intimacy established upon the
fact of a common residence at Craig's Cross,
and the laughingly acknowledged bond of
"our road."   She had accepted this state of
affairs with scarcely a thought concerning it
then, but now, suddenly revived after these
quiet months at home, it jarred upon her.
There seemed in the assured confident manner
the slightest possible hint of a proprietorship
in herself as well as in the road.   She had

never noticed anything of the kind before, but the idea, once suggested, recurred unpleasantly, and could not be wholly shaken off. It might have been either the cause or the effect of her new involuntary recoil from the old tone of familiar acquaintanceship. She did not question concerning it: she was only conscious of the scarcely defined feeling of constraint and repulsion.

Meanwhile the others were chatting animatedly of common interests and acquaintances, while they established themselves comfortably in the newest and most luxurious car, to which they had been at once deferentially directed. Meeting Mr. Corry was like a breath from the living, moving world again, Nan declared with her most gracious *empressement*.

"And one needs such a breath occasionally in this sleepy little town. Uncle Lyndal's place is lovely, but so still, and your father's beautiful new residence — it seems almost a waste to build it here, only, of course, the demands of his business make that imperative."

Rachel wondered, scanning for a moment his smiling face as he replied, whether he knew what other voices, those of which she had heard yesterday, were saying of that house. Probably the murmurings were too cautious and timid to reach his ears, but was it possible that he knew of the wrong? Even then he might be powerless to prevent it — as powerless as herself, she reflected with a sudden flush sweeping over her face. A little later the train paused for a few minutes at a way station, and he left the car. He was recognized, evidently, as he passed here and there, and presently they saw a man approach eagerly and engage him in conversation.

"What a contrast between those two men!" commented Nan as she watched them from the window. "How plainly the vast difference in station, education, refinement and culture betrays itself in the faces and in every attitude and gesture, though we do not hear a word they utter!"

A young man, bronzed and bearded, wearing the common dress of a workman, was talking rapidly and earnestly, — somewhat anxiously, it seemed to Rachel, as she noted the eager look and quick movement. Opposite him Mr. Corry's fine figure in the careless perfection of its attire, and his cool handsome face, certainly showed to advantage. In sharp contrast, too, was his half-amused, half-indifferent air as he listened, and the smile of good-natured tolerance with which he finally accepted a paper offered him, ran over its contents, and drawing out his pocket-book gave something in exchange for it. The whistle sounded its quick summons, and he placed book and paper in his pocket, and returned in the leisurely fashion of one for whom even time and tide must wait, to his place.

"You combine business and pleasure?" Nan questioned.

"Oh, I am obliged to do that," he laughed. "These fellows are always wanting something, and they keep too sharp a watch for any one from the office to allow us to pass unnoticed. They are a thriftless, improvident set, earning their wages, and then willing to throw away a goodly slice of them in their hurry to get their money a little sooner than the regular pay-day."

"But is the pay-day regular?" Rachel asked. "I thought — at least I have heard — that it is often delayed, and that the workmen scarcely know when to expect it."

"Well, there are delays, of course," Mr. Corry admitted; "that is unavoidable at times. But the paymaster's car is sure to come, they have no doubt of that, only they are so eager to spend as fast or a little faster than they earn, that they haven't patience to wait. And fifty cents to-day looks larger than a dollar to-morrow."

"Then when you buy their time — that is

what they call it, I believe — you do not pay them its full value?" Rachel hesitated a moment before she asked this question, nerving herself to meet the answer from which she shrank. But it did not disturb Mr. Corry.

"Certainly not," he replied promptly. "If a man has not sense, patience or frugality enough to wait until he can fairly reap the fruit of his labor, he must take the loss his haste or folly brings. Is not that just, Miss Lisle?"

"I am inclined to think it is kind also," Nan assented. "In my opinion, the surest method of making people choose better ways is not by helping them in their own miserable one, but by allowing them to feel its discomforts so keenly that they will be forced to seek some plan of improvement." A smiling glance at Rachel pointed the sentence.

But Rachel's grave eyes were turned to the window again, where the smoke of the flying train threw faint shadows over the hillside.

She did not pursue the subject, but her thoughts, could Mr. Corry have read them, might have slightly disturbed his complacent composure.

A half hour's ride brought another halt. Large quantities of stone had been brought from a quarry near by for the building of a bridge, and the party left the car to view the work. One of the workmen, fumbling about among the stones in awkward pretence of searching for something lost, contrived to draw near enough to speak to Rachel unheard by the others. Until he addressed her she did not recognize in his working garb the young Irishman whom she had seen the day before.

"If ye plaze, miss, mebby I was a bit free wid me tongue yestherday — talkin' of some folks, ye know," he said, with a significant apprehensive glance in the direction of her companions. "Sure ye wouldn't mintion it where 'twould harm me at all? I'd not like to be losin' me place these times, 'count o' them," with a nod towards one of the little cabins on the hillside.

Under his effort to speak carelessly there was such evident anxiety that she answered at once, —

"Certainly not." Then with a flitting smile, "I will be silent if you are. You must not send others to me with any hope that I can do for them what I did for you — I cannot."

"Sure ye can't, Miss. I'd not be expectin' it," he answered with quick comprehension. Yet his look of relief at her promise was followed by a shade of disappointment, as if some hope had been quenched.

Something, a desire to hear an answer from this man's standpoint, prompted her to say, —

"I am told that Mr. Corry thinks the men need not sell their time if they were more careful and patient; that they are in haste to spend what they earn, and so consider fifty cents to-day worth more than a dollar to-morrow."

A queer look passed over the rough face. There was a muttered word smothered in its articulation, and then he replied with grim quietness, —

"When a man's child is sick he's like enough to think the fifty cents to buy it medicine to-day is better than two dollars to bury it to-morrow when he's seen it die for want of help. Misther Corry is right, ma'am; he giner'ly is. An' it's patience we're wantin'! Faith, it's a fine chance to learn it on this road. Beggin' yer parding, ma'am" — with another quick remembrance of whom he was addressing.

The girl remembered also, with a sudden flush, that was neither pride nor pleasure, as she turned away.

"Another of your acquaintances?" questioned Miss Lisle with a slight arching of her eyebrows.

But Rachel did not explain. She noticed with new interest and deeper thought, that

day, the cabins clustered here and there along
the road—"our road." The feeling of proprietorship that had been so gratifying to her
girlish fancy was beginning to assume new
aspects, and bring its burdens now. A sense
of responsibility still clung to her even through
the dawning knowledge of her helplessness to
right the wrongs she saw; and through all
those bright hours she puzzled her young
heart and brain with the tangled questions
that have perplexed and saddened so many
older, wiser ones—why the rich man's flocks
and herds must be spared and the poor man's
one ewe-lamb be sacrificed? Why Dives
must be allowed to enjoy his feast though
Lazarus starved at the gate?

"Cousin Heman," she said one evening
when, out on the moonlit veranda, he and
Miss Lisle had been discoursing eloquently —
it was a subject upon which Miss Lisle was
always eloquent—of the life-work he had
chosen, "what would you do if, instead of the

city congregations you know, your parish should be entirely different—made up of such people as these in the shops and along the line? What would you teach them?   How help them?"   There was some curiosity in the question, but more of wistful earnestness.

"An improbable and not very flattering supposition," remarked Nan rather resentfully. "Heman's talents will at least prevent his burial in any obscure corner, I fancy."

"Well," answered the young gentleman, slowly considering the subject, as if, however, such consideration were new to him, "if I were so situated I should try to do my best for them, of course, — the gospel is for all, — and to adapt myself to their comprehension."

"And to inculcate industry, sobriety and contentment with their station," suggested Nan. "I think that is one great need of the poorer classes — to learn contentment with their lot."

"Certainly — the very teaching most needed

by these classes." He brushed a fallen rose-leaf from his sleeve of immaculate broadcloth. "Certainly."

Classes! Rachel wondered if they stood before his mental vision all accurately graded and nicely labelled! He would preach to them only as "classes:" as individual souls, each with its own separate life, its peculiar temptations and burdens, he would never know them. The varied natures, upreaching, hungering, struggling; the tired, sensitive hearts, crushed by poverty and failure; the strong spirits, maddened by wrong, or made bitter and faithless by seeing others fling away what would be life to them and theirs, — all this he would never understand; to such he would bring no gospel of hope, patience or strength.

"I hope you will have your wealthy city congregation," she said with a long breath.

"Little doubt of that," answered Nan loftily, "though," she added with a sudden suspicion that some sarcasm might have lurked under the adjectives, "he will expect to find some poor — even the very poor — in his parish, of course, since they are everywhere. But they will not be dealt with — at least I should not deal with such persons as you do, Rachel. It is no kindness to pretend that they are upon your own level. I would bestow charity, indeed, but I should think it my duty to accompany it with good advice and careful oversight."

"Yes, I am not good at that, Nan," laughed Rachel at thought of her cousin bestowing her wise and proper benefactions upon Mrs. Shackles, or Joe Baines — whom she had seen once or twice since his first appearance. Yet something in the same thought gathered the tears for an instant under her lashes. "If I were a believer in pre-existence, I should fancy I had sometime been a poor vagabond or outcast myself," she said, "for they touch a spot in my heart that seems sore, as if from some unremembered experience."

A heathenish creed and preposterous fancy,

Miss Lisle's wide-open eyes said — one of the constantly recurring proofs of Rachel's oddity. But she and Mr. Weldon dropped at once into a discussion of, or rather conversation upon, Plato, and afterwards the ancient Egyptians, who, being conveniently dead, could be classified and disposed of in a proper, comfortable way, impossible to these troublesome living subjects.

Rachel wandered away from their mild metaphysical deductions, down the white gravelled walk to the arched gateway. Looking away down the slope to the river, her gaze was suddenly recalled.

"If you please, marm, here's the twins," said Joe Baines in a voice of unmistakable delight, drawing into the full moonlight that fell on the road, two queer, tiny figures that appeared to be only faded aprons surmounted by coarse flopping hats. "Why, Joe!" exclaimed Rachel, startled, then laughing. "These babies ought to be in bed!"

"Yes, marm, they mostly do be this time," explained Joe. "But you see, I don't get no time only nights, and 'twas early yet, and moony, so I thought I'd bring 'em round this way, and mebby you'd be out somewheres so's you'd get a look at 'em. 'Most thought we'd have to give it up, though, 'thout seein' ye," he added with a sigh of satisfaction at the success that had crowned his effort.

Joe had obtained work in the yards. "Cæsar did but carelessly nod on him," and the coveted situation was found for him at once. He was wondrously contented, and cherished an almost worshipful admiration for the " big Judge's darter."

"Ain't they fine fellows, now?" he questioned exultingly, pushing the children nearer. "Take off your hats, twins, and bow to the lady."

Two spasmodic jerks of the two straw extinguishers followed, and two round tow-heads were revealed.

" Very fine boys indeed, Joe," said Rachel appreciatingly. "What are their names?"

"Nip and Tuck, marm. You see when Meg first left 'em they was that little that some sickness was always a-happenin' to 'em, till it seemed 'sif first one'd die, an' then 'sif t'other'd die, an' so we got to callin' 'em that. Josier an' Dan'l they be really, but they don't know nothin' 'bout that. Ain't they grown fine? Oh, we'll get along now, marm!"

Rachel praised the round healthful cheeks, and filled the chubby hands with grapes, and Joe turned away with his charge, his heavy face lighted by more than moonbeams.

Out of the town, away in a wide green meadow by the roadside, stood an old railway-car that, long unused, had lately been drawn up there under the shade of a great oak tree, and fitted up, in rude fashion, for a habitation. Weather-beaten and somewhat dilapidated, it yet bore marks of recent patching, and there had been a rough shanty-like addition built at the back, from the roof of which a rusty piece of stove-pipe protruded, proclaiming the kitchen of the establishment. Inside the car itself a partition had been put up, dividing the once long, narrow apartment into two smaller ones. The seats had nearly all been removed long before it had fallen to its present occupation, but a dilapidated one, carefully propped up, remained at each end of the main apartment, and these, with their faded velvet cushions, were the especial pride of the small mistress of the place, since her domain had little other furnishing.

An odd little figure was she, in coarse dress, almost as much too long for her as it was too old in style for her twelve or thirteen years, and the small grave face, with its great gray eyes, wore a look of precocious womanliness. There was a care-taking, matronly air in all her movements too, as she stood for a moment, with hand shading her eyes, looking anxiously from the door, and then, turning away, placed thread and needle upon the table, and seated herself with a basket of mending.

The room had one other occupant — an old, feeble, white-haired man, holding a violin whose strings he touched occasionally. "Fiddling Simon" was rapidly becoming known in the town and adjacent country, walking as far as his strength would permit, playing here and there, picking up what pence he could, but scrupulously spending it all for lottery tickets from which he always expected to reap a fortune. Disappointed again and again, he grew only more confident by failure, and the one joy of his life was to talk of his prospective prizes and the wealth they would bring.

"Hitty, don't you s'pose it'll come to-morrer —or next week, mebby?" he asked, as he was always asking.

"Mebby, Daddy," answered Hitty with thoughts intent upon her work.

"And then I'll have a new fiddle and clo'es —we'll all have clo'es — and a house with"—

"Yes," said Hitty absently, her little red hands awkwardly drawing rents together, and fitting on odd pieces, while a perplexed wrinkle deepened now and then in her unchildlike forehead.

"A fine big house with — with — what'll we have in it, Hitty?" querulously.

"Carpets and sofys and pianers," began the little woman in the tone of one repeating a familiar lesson. "There! that's crooked — and pictures — how will I fix that patch?"

"Hitty, I don't want so many patches in it!" expostulated the old man impatiently.

"No, no, Daddy! we won't have none in it! It's pictures I meant — pictures," explained Hitty soothingly.

"An' carriages an' horses. You don't tell nothin' 'bout them; you used to know all 'bout them."

"Horses and velvety carriages with lamps to 'em," added the patient young seamstress, enumerating the prospective grandeurs with matter-of-fact tone, and brows still knitted over her patching.

There was a shuffling heavy step outside, then a scrambling of children's feet, and Joe appeared with the twins. Hitty looked up relieved, but her observation was quiet enough :

"You did be a long time, Joe."

"Yes, it took a waitin', but she's seen 'em, Hitty — she's seen them twins ! I got 'em right where she could look at 'em square," answered Joe exultingly, as if such consummation were worth years of waiting.

The same feeling seemed to linger long after Hitty, moving about in her grave and housewifely fashion, had disposed of the children for the night, and returned to her work. He viewed with satisfaction her awkward darning and odd drawing together of rents.

"You're a master hand at patchin', Hitty. Oh, we're gettin' along now, I tell you, since she got me a place to work — the Judge's darter. Some day we'll fix up like folks, if we keep on, and buy them twins some gor-ge-ous aperns! I've seen the stuff in the stores, and I've kept a thinkin'. Red and blue and posies all over it!"

"And, Joe," said Hitty, with thoughts going deeper than his, "mebby, some day, when they get bigger and we get on, we can send em' where they'll get learnin'?"

"Sure! we'll have 'em know all what's in books, Hitty."

"'Cause I think that's what makes folks like — like folks," she said slowly, failing to find any words to express the sense of some great difference between herself and others that she had often felt but did not understand. "Mebby they can tell us some, after a while, Joe?" wistfully.

"They'll be fine fellers, them twins," affirmed Joe, shaking his bushy head solemnly. "Wouldn't Meg say we'd done our level best if she could see 'em with them new aperns?"

CHAPTER IV.

THE DOCTOR'S HOLIDAY.

HEMAN laid an open letter on the table beside him, and looked at Rachel with a smile.

"I shall have an opportunity of answering practically your question of a few evenings ago."

"What was it? I did not know I had asked one worth remembering so long."

"You asked what I would preach to a congregation made up of such people as those about Craig's Cross. It seems the city pastors have been holding a series of evening meetings in a school-house some five or six miles from here, each taking charge of it in turn. Dr. Lowe, to whose lot it falls this week, is unable to come, and, hearing that I was in the neighborhood, has written asking me to take his place."

" Ah, yes, I recollect hearing something about that," said the Judge, drawing on his gloves, and glancing from his watch to the window for his carriage to make its appearance. " Out at Gill's school-house. It is not very far by a direct route over the hills, but five or six miles, I suppose, by the only decent carriage road. However, that will not matter much these bright moonlight nights. I presume the girls will go also ; it is really a rather pleasant drive out there, and you will all enjoy it. Do your best for that meeting, Heman. They are a set that need preaching to badly enough." And the Judge laughed and hurried away.

One of the girls expressed her approval of the plan so heartily that her enthusiasm fortunately covered the slightly hesitating acquiescence of the other. Rachel's pleasure in the purpose of the expedition was not unqualified, nor did it grow more so when, later in the day, she heard Nan, in conversation with Mr. Corry, explaining their engagement for the next evening. His knowledge of the locality in question, and his expressions of interest in the project, ended very naturally in his joining the party At least it seemed a very natural and most satisfactory arrangement to both Annice and Heman, and Rachel could not refuse to second the invitation.

"Mr. Corry is so genial, so sensible and practical, that he is always an agreeable acquisition," Miss Lisle remarked to her cousin afterwards, with the air of one whose opinion upon such a subject settled it beyond all controversy. It was seemingly allowed to do so. Rachel made no reply.

A respectable audience in point of numbers —and it was quiet and orderly also — had gathered in the plain, dimly lighted little building by the time the carriage arrived.

"If he's a-goin' to preach the Gospil, I'm a-goin' to be there to hear it, 'cause I don't go to

meetin's often, 'count of havin' no clo'es an
things to go with," Mrs. Shackles had observed
to Humphrey; and others had apparently been
of her opinion. Joe Baines, Hitty and the
twins were there — a result that had taxed
Hitty's powers of preparation to the utmost,
and cost Joe an evening of grave planning.
The idea had first occurred to him from a bit
of talk overheard at the yard. Joe heard
many things in that way, seldom talking to
the men, or they to him, as he went, day after
day, about his work in his dull, heavy, but
steady, fashion, not comprehending many of
their familiar topics, but wondering and pondering often in his slow brain. But this was
an item of intelligence that had suddenly assumed a possible practical interest to himself,
and he explained at home what he had heard
as clearly as he understood it.

"So it's more'n like she'll be there, 'cause
he's her cousin. And we'll fix up and go,
Hitty, and take them twins; an' she'll see all

of us a-hearin' of him!" concluded Joe, reaching his grand culmination impressively.

It was a great undertaking, but it was successfully carried out. Hitty had done her luckless best — poor tired little seamstress! — and, arrayed in marvellous proofs of her industry, they occupied a front seat when the party from Judge Lyndal's arrived. They were not disappointed. Joe, earnestly watching for it, did not miss a pleasant glance of recognition from the Judge's daughter, though the corners of her mouth quivered for a moment as she looked in that direction.

Nan, scanning the congregation and then the young minister, thought proudly how out of place he seemed among them. Rachel thought the same thing, though without the pride, and for a different reason. A moment later she started at an unexpected presence. Dr. Kelsey walked quietly into the room, and sought a retired seat among the listeners. Nan looked a mute interrogation at her cousin.

There was opportunity for nothing more, for Heman was already standing by the plain deal table which served as a desk, and Rachel, with a curious mingling of hope and misgiving, turned resolutely from other thoughts to hear for herself what he had to say to "this class of people."

There was a description of the dangers and temptations of wealth, and the folly of making its acquirement a chief aim in life, or of supposing that its possession could bring happiness; a poetical picture of contented poverty, fashioned after the "Cotter's Saturday Night." The evils of discontent and envy were portrayed, with a rather vague and abstruse warning against communism and kindred madnesses; and many truths and half truths, mingled with some wholesome and some very doubtful deductions, were set forth in choice language. There was much about the different allotments of life as of God's appointment, but very little about the Carpenter of Nazareth, who became such for our sakes, and "was tempted in all points like as we are" — the Brother and the Lord in one, who went out with the fishermen, and could fill the nets to overflowing when he willed; who had power to make the few loaves many, and the greater power still to make fasting with Him seem sweeter than feasting elsewhere, and a home in His promised kingdom worth counting all earthly things loss to win.

Missing this, Rachel wondered, looking on the faces around her — keen, intelligent faces, many of them — what they thought of it all. There was a listlessness with some, a growing restlessness with others, as the address drew to a close; and the instant the speaker ceased, a rough-looking man, drawing a long breath that might possibly been one of relief, began to sing, without waiting for any hymn to be announced, —

> " We're going home, no more to roam
>   No more to sin and sorrow;
> No more to wear the brow of care —
>   We're going home to-morrow.

" For weary feet awaits the street
    All wondrous paved and golden;
For hearts that ache. the angels wake
    The story sweet and olden.
        We're going home, we're going home,
        We're going home to-morrow."

In a moment the air of lassitude and weari-
ness had vanished, and the people joined in the
song with an energy and power that added
depth and meaning to the words. It was the
homesick longing of souls that had found the
way hard. Miss Lisle's fair, delicate face
betrayed surprise, annoyance, and the faintest
perceptible shade of disgust. Mr. Corry
watched the scene curiously, but Rachel, turning a little away from both faces, after a moment or two sang softly with the others.

There was a brief awkward pause when the
singing ended. Mr. Weldon did not know
what next to expect, but as nothing came he
closed the meeting, the people passed out, and
our party made their way to the carriage almost
in silence. The promised moonlight had failed

to appear, and in its stead were heavy clouds which presently deepened to rain.

"It seems to me," said Nan in an injured tone, "that the city ministers are expending a great deal of labor for a very small return in coming out here every week."

"Especially if they depend upon the moon-light," laughed Mr. Corry. "Still, it was not a bad audience — in quantity, whatever may be said of its quality."

Mr. Weldon prudently refrained from expressing an opinion. He was beginning to have a glimmering suspicion of the reason why missionaries must often remain so long among their particular branch of heathen before they are able to do any efficient work. He had certainly considered his address very satisfactory when he had prepared it the previous day, and rehearsed it to the well-bred stuffed chairs in his room, and he could not quite account for the sense of discomfort that assailed him now. He pondered the subject during the first mile of the homeward ride, and then meditation and journey came to an abrupt halt together. There was a sudden jar and jolt, the carriage lunged and tipped, and the driver sprang from his seat in time narrowly to escape being thrown from it.

"Halloo! What's wrong?"

The gentlemen clambered out as the horses stopped, — alighting was not easy in the position the vehicle had assumed, — and assisted the ladies to do the same. At that moment a horseman joined them, and Dr. Kelsey's voice inquired the cause of the trouble

"Something wrong with the carriage; I can't discover what, in this light — or rather in the want of it," answered Mr. Corry, peering at the oddly tangled wheels.

"Something that'll keep it from going any further this night, or I'm mistaken," muttered the coachman. .

Nan moved her foot impatiently on the wet ground. It was not a pleasant place for standing, and the slow rain was changing to a brisk shower.

"This is a fine location for a break-down," she commented.

"There is a farm-house a little way back from the road where we can find shelter for the ladies," suggested the doctor. "And probably we can borrow a lantern, and so discover the exact extent of the damage, and what can be done about it."

"Commend me to a surgeon for sensible advice in all cases of fracture!" declared Mr. Corry in a tone of relief. "I did not know there was a house in the vicinity. Lead the way, Doctor, and we will follow."

The doctor offered his arm to Rachel.

"It will be an uncomfortable walk up a rough muddy lane, but it is not a long one."

The whole party contrived to find considerable merriment in it, though they presented a forlornly draggled appearance when the light from the open door flashed out upon them.   A poor, plain little farm-house it was, but it offered a ready, if somewhat uncouth, hospitality.

The farmer produced a lantern, and enlisted in the service at once, while his wife lighted a fire in the open grate in the best room, remarking that it was "a real chill rain, and an open fire dries damp clothes the fastest, anyhow."

"How cheery!" exclaimed Rachel, settling her feet on the fender and watching the bright blaze as it lighted up the whitewashed walls

"For us, but not for the others out in the rain," replied Nan reprovingly.

They soon returned, however, to report the impossibility of using the carriage that night, and to take counsel as to the course to be pursued under the circumstances.

"Mr. Weldon and yourself might take the horses and ride back to Craig's Cross," said the doctor, turning to Mr. Corry.

"Only that it seems useless for two of us to go," interposed Heman.

" And in that way you could secure another conveyance in the town while he might ride directly to Judge Lyndal's, procure extra wraps for the ladies, and explain the cause of the delay to Mrs. Lyndal so that she need suffer no alarm. It is important that she should not," proceeded the doctor quietly, without seeming to have heard the interruption.

" And the ladies, meanwhile? " questioned Mr. Corry, a trifle discontentedly.

" Can remain here. I have a patient to visit up on the hillside road, but I will wait until you return."

It was a very sensible arrangement, yet neither of the gentlemen addressed looked particularly well pleased with it. There seemed no good reason for demurring, however, especially as Miss Lyndal promptly approved it and her cousin did not object ; so the plan was accepted, and the two rode away upon their mission.

" Now," said the doctor, turning from the door where he had watched their departure, "we shall have about two hours of waiting, in which we must try to make ourselves as comfortable as possible."

His look and tone said that he expected to be exceedingly comfortable. His manner, indeed, was not unlike that of a school-boy who finds himself in possession of an unexpected holiday. He stirred the fire to a brighter blaze, and drew two stiff wooden rocking-chairs from obscure corners to a pleasanter position.

"They are the nearest approach to luxury the place affords," he said as he arranged them. "And I suppose it is our duty to be content with them, if we are to practise the teachings Mr. Weldon gave us this day," he added mischievously as he saw the look which Nan bestowed upon the gayly painted misfitting back and creaking rockers, as she accepted the chair he offered.

"We were surprised to see you in such an out-of-the way place as that little school-house," said Rachel, recurring to her wonder of early in the evening. "You have not told us how it happened."

"I had a visit to make in this direction, as I said a few minutes ago. I heard of the meeting and stopped there," the doctor explained indefinitely. His attendance might or might not have been in a measure accidental.

"I trust that case of illness is not a very serious one, since we are so unfortunately delaying your call," remarked Nan rather stiffly. Heman's sermons were well enough, of course, but she did not enjoy any hint that she was expected to practise them in the way of foregoing luxuries and submitting to inconveniences. The suggestion, from such a source, savored of presumption !

" I trust it is not," the doctor responded serenely.

He did not seem at all uneasy about it or disturbed by the delay. When the fire was dancing and sparkling to his satisfaction, he

sought the kitchen and the hostess, who was
knitting and hospitably trying to keep awake
while her guests remained, and entered into a
secret consultation with her concerning the
capabilities of her cellar and dairy — combining a few adroitly managed suggestions with
a judicious tender of ample compensation for
extra trouble. He appeared so thoroughly and
enjoyably at ease, so perfectly at home in this
unexpected situation, that Nan slightly resent-
ed it.   It was very pleasant, under the circumstances, to have him there, and to have
him so considerate and agreeable ; but considering the company in which he found himself,
it did seem as if a more abashed and reverent
manner, a little more of admiring awe, might
have been expected from this mere country
doctor. It suddenly occurred to her that these
plain homely surroundings might have something to do with the change — for there certainly was a change from his usual reserved
professional demeanor. Very possibly he felt

himself in a more familiar and natural atmosphere here than in Judge Lyndal's parlors,
and other places of their occasional meeting.

"But it is strange how people can live on
year after year in such a way and with such
surroundings," she said, uttering her concluding thought aloud as she glanced at the placid
pink-and-white faces of "Henry" and "Rosalie"
which in glaring water-colors and cheap frames
adorned the walls.

"There is nothing very difficult about it,
Miss Lisle, nor very distressing either," asserted the doctor. "I speak from experience, for
I grew up from boyhood in a farm-house but
little larger than this, and not any more luxurious. There was a large family of us, boys
and girls, and I do assure you we had no idea
that we were enduring martyrdom. No," he
laughed as he followed Nan's glance toward
the pictures again, "we did not possess those
gorgeous works of art, but I have no doubt we
should have enjoyed them. Our masterpieces

were a bird chalked on the barn-door by a neighbor, and a few cuts clipped from almanacs and stray papers, and pasted on the walls of the room we boys occupied — a chamber with a sloping ceiling, Miss Lisle; and the height of our ambition was to grow tall enough to bump our heads against it."

How audacious he was in the very face of her disdain! She half enjoyed it herself, and that Rachel did so wholly, her dancing eyes testified. "Children are easily satisfied," vouchsafed Miss Lisle more graciously than might have been expected.

"But I even find it very pleasant, cosey and homelike now, when I go back for a visit, as I often do," the doctor persisted, but with a momentary softening of his tone, as if some tender memory touched it.

"One's friends and home, of course — " began Nan, and then left the sentence unfinished because she could think of no relevant conclusion — an awkwardness very unusual with her.

In revenge for having been forced into it, she ostensibly changed the subject, spoke of some late magazine sketches on rural life, and glided from thence to books and authors, appealing to the doctor's knowledge of this and his opinion of that. She intended to reveal to him in a seemingly unconscious way the superior advantages he had missed. But apparently he had missed very few. She was surprised, though no glance or inflection betrayed it. She dexterously turned to popular lectures. That was more successful. He listened with interest to her glowing descriptions, and asked some questions concerning the topics and their treatment, that were not easily answered — at least to her own satisfaction; but he owned, without the slightest trace of embarrassment or envy, that he had never heard them.

"There has not been time, since Craig's Cross does not attract stars of such magnitude. I am trying to cultivate the grace of being satisfied to leave some desirable things undone.

In Methuselah's time people must have had a grand chance to do the world thoroughly ; but now life is not long enough."

Some words about "judging our lives by what we allow to be crowded out of them " flashed through Rachel's thought, but Nan only smiled, and her evenly modulated voice went on :

"Then I suppose that philosophy has consoled you for missing some of our great actors and dramas also?   It is almost a pity it should have done so.   Not that one cares to bestow a too frequent or indiscriminate attendance upon even the so-called best "— she guarded her remark with a proper remembrance of her future position, and with a haste which seemed to embody some fear that the gentleman before her might immediately begin to squander his time and vitiate his taste if he were not duly warned.   "But some are really pure and elevating.   They delineate a lofty heroism and nobility of character that can scarcely be witnessed elsewhere — a truly grand ideal."

"I do not know," said the doctor reflectively, less as if he were answering her than pondering the subject for his own satisfaction. "I think many of the 'grand deeds,' robbed of their dress, the lights and the general glamour of the surroundings, are not so very uncommon. Take Richelieu's much-admired defence of his ward. Why, I could find a dozen men, any day, on almost any street — men carrying prosaic dinner-pails, and going to the most commonplace work — who would do as much for a defenceless girl, and then go quietly on their way without rolling their eyes or their R's in making high-sounding speeches about it. Neither they nor any one else would think that they had done anything remarkable."

Dr. Kelsey could scarcely have known how aggravating he was. Fortunately, the result of his negotiation with the farmer's wife became speedily apparent in the spreading of a neat little table, and its furnishing with an array of tempting country dainties that were enjoyable after the long ride and the cool breeze. Through the open door came the sound of the steadily falling rain. Inside, the fire threw its glow over the rag carpet, the braided mats and the white walls, glistening the plain table service, and lighting up the faces gathered around it.

"It seems like a chapter out of some other book — as if we had stolen a few leaves from a story not our own," said Rachel, surveying her surroundings.

"I hope it is not to be continued," commented Annice, with a slight shrug of the graceful shoulders around which she had thrown a very becoming white shawl. She was looking extremely well. Even an old-fashioned mirror, decorated with peacock-plumes and nodding asparagus-berries, could tell that, and her brow smoothed as she caught the reflection.

Rachel laughed softly. She did not echo her cousin's hope, audibly at least, the doctor noticed, and she seemed charmingly resigned. A faint flush came to her cheeks and a brighter light to her eyes. She lured the gentleman into a description of the little frame country school-house where his education began, and of the delights of school-teaching with which he had been obliged to diversify his college course. One might have fancied she found a mischievous enjoyment in shocking Miss Lisle's high opinions and prejudices. Perhaps Dr. Kelsey had a motive of his own for softening no rugged outline of the sketches he gave, for allowing the struggle and poverty of earlier years, though not vaunted, to stand unconcealed. In any case, Miss Lyndal did not appear appalled. The mirthful light in her eyes softened sometimes, that was all. The whole incomprehensible proceeding was of a piece with her toleration of that horrible Mrs. Shackles and her other odd protégés, Nan decided, leaning back in her chair and watching her two companions with a little motion of her delicate fingers as if she were secretly washing her hands of them.

However, the man could talk remarkably well, she admitted that. Of course he was a monument of wasted possibilities, but since she was not responsible she need not refuse to be entertained; and having reached this sensible conclusion, she grew more affable again, and had forgotten to watch the clock, when the sound of carriage-wheels startled her.

"They are coming!" she said, looking from the window.

"Did you think we were forever and a day on our mission?" demanded Mr. Corry cheerily. "It seemed so to us, I assure you. And by the way, Doctor, we are bound to confess that we discovered the wisdom of your suggestion that two could divide the labor and expedite the return."

Dr. Kelsey bowed silently. Perhaps he began to doubt his own wisdom in the arrangement. He sought the farmer and his wife while the party made their hasty preparations for departure, and the darkness hid his grave face as he assisted the ladies into the carriage and turned away with a quietly courteous " good-night." Then he mounted his horse, drew his hat low over his eyes, and plunged into the rain and gloom in an opposite direction. He had had his holiday, and it was over.

CHAPTER V.

NOT WHOLLY SATISFACTORY.

NEEDN'T nobody tell me that a meetin' ain't no use, even if 'tain't a partic'lar good one!" declared Mrs. Shackles. She considered that she had reaped substantial benefit by finding in the road the next day a scarf which she recognized as Miss Lyndal's. It was wet and spoiled by the rain, but who could say that honesty did not require her to return it? And that furnished a laudable reason for visiting the great house on the hill — no insignificant matter, in what the old woman called " a dry fortnight betwixt berries."

So, a morning or two later, she set out to restore the bit of lost property, plodding through the hot sun, and mentally recounting all the toils and fatigues she was undergoing, that she might have them in readiness to relate, and so enhance the value of her service. When she reached the house, however, no one was visible on the piazza or through the front windows; and after a long and careful scrutiny she was reluctantly obliged to modify her plan and walk around the house. With Miss Rachel not in sight, "Peggy Larrison," as she denominated the housekeeper, would never forgive her for summoning any one to the front door. She hesitated a moment on the steps, looking into the wide inviting kitchen.

"I s'pose Miss Lyndal ain't home?" she remarked interrogatively.

"I suppose she isn't," replied the housekeeper dryly, startled by the voice, and a trifle vexed when she discovered the intruder. "You wouldn't have come to this door if she had been."

"No more I wouldn't," declared Mrs. Shackles stoutly, "for I wanted to see her 'bout something partic'lar."

A rosy-cheeked maiden, with sleeves rolled above her plump elbows, giggled, and remarked in an audible aside that it was "a pity Miss Rachel hadn't known."

"If it is a very important message you might leave it with me, and I'll deliver it as soon as she comes in," suggested Mrs. Larrison, amused at the evident dissatisfaction her proposal called forth.

"'Tain't just a message. It's something she's lost, and I'm clear beat out bringin' it back through this hot sun. I s'pose I'll have to come ag'in, though."

Whereupon she was invited to enter, and Rosy-cheeks, by direction, brought her a glass of milk, though the pert damsel tittered again when the stained and road-soiled scarf was displayed, and hazarded the remark that "Miss Rachel might have been able to do without it till sunset, if it was such very hard work to bring it back in the heat of the day."

"Well, it was," responded the old woman

severely, " with no better par'sol to keep the sun
off'n this old slitted one. An' I s'pose pretty
soon I'll have none, 'cause I hain't got no prospeck of buyin' none, an' I won't beg for nobody.
But, as I tells Humphrey, I guess I'm honest
enough to take things back to their owners if
I do br'il my head a-doin' it."

" I presume I can find a light umbrella that
you can have, if that is what you want,"
answered the housekeeper. She was kind-
hearted, and if she lacked patience with her
visitor, she had a boundless affection for Miss
Rachel and a due regard for all her whims.

Fairly seated, and with such an auspicious
opening, Mrs. Shackles was in no haste to
depart. She settled herself comfortably, dis-
coursed of the berry crop, and gave her opinion of the meeting she had attended.

" Oh, he talked about the Frinch revolution
— I know it's the style to bring 'most everything from the Frinch nowadays, but I didn't
know our own revolution had gone out o' fash-

ion. My father he fit in it, and most folks
thought 'twould last if 'twas home-made.
Then he talked about the communion — whatever that may be — and the ile-ists, though
dear knows nobody ever struck ile in these
parts! I s'pose mebby he writ that sermon for
somewhere else, though, an' hadn't time to
make it over; it didn't seem to fit somehow.
'Tain't his fault that he's been shut up in one
of them theology cemeteries till he don't know
nothin' how to talk to folks — I don't mean
people, I mean folks — real human critters!
He'll preach at 'em enough, but he'll never
preach to 'em, 'cause they won't be there
— land sakes, no! not within miles of where
he's aimin' at."

"If Mr. Weldon's sermon wasn't appreciated
it's not likely the fault was in the preacher,"
interposed Mrs. Larrison stiffly. She did not
relish any criticism of the family. "He is a
young man yet, and I daresay he will make
a fine minister. Most people grow wiser as

they grow older. Here is that small umbrella and a can of milk — if you are going now."

Mrs. Shackles perceived that she had introduced an unfortunate topic, and she accepted the gift and her dismissal with tolerable grace.

" Yes," she remarked for her own edification as she slowly wended her way around the house, "folks does grow wiser — some of 'em. But he ain't one of the kind of cakes that'll ever rise an' run over; he'll al'ays stay nice and smooth in the same little pan he was first mixed in."

As she turned the corner and passed out upon the gravelled walk her dim eyes brightened. Through the open window she caught the flutter of a light dress, the glimpse of a flitting figure in the shadowy distance of the apartment. Miss Rachel was at home after all, and she would see her " in spite of Peggy Larrison or any of 'em." With this valiant determination she entered hastily, and not until she had uttered her customary " Mornin' ! "

and dropped down upon a chair near the door, did she discover, in the softened light of the room, that she had made a mistake and was confronting not Miss Lyndal but her cousin.

"Sakes! it's you!" she exclaimed with a scarcely flattering emphasis upon the pronoun. "I 'most wonder I couldn't 'a' told that if it does seem nigh about as dark as Egypt here, just comin' in from the light. Miss Rachel ain't to home, I s'pose?"

Nan was secretly glad of the encounter. There were a few things that this obtrusive old woman needed to be taught, and she had no doubt of her own eminent fitness to teach them.

"What did you want of Miss Lyndal?" she asked.

"Why, she dropped her scarf out o' the carriage t'other night — rich folks al'ays does have more'n they can rightly hold on to — an' I've travelled all this way through the blazin', br'ilin' sun to bring it back to her."

"That is all very well," said Miss Lisle

judicially, "but, my good woman, don't you
think it would appear better for you to go to
the back door when you come to Judge Lyndal's house?"

"'Pear better?" Mrs. Shackles scrutinized
the fair face opposite her as if she entertained
some doubt whether she had heard correctly.
"Sakes! no! Leastways I ain't so partic'lar
'bout my 'pearance as some folks. 'Handsome
is as handsome does,' I tells Humphrey when
he says what old bunnits I wear, an' no prospeck of gettin' better. I ain't so stuck up
'bout my looks as some folks, though I don't
mind ownin' I'd like a new bunnit. But nobody knows it, for I ain't one of the beggin'
kind, nor never will be. Only if anybody
offers things that fit I ain't too proud to take 'em.
Seems like that's what we was put into this
world for — to help one another — an' I ain't
goin' to hender nobody from doin' their duty,
by not takin' what's offered. My head's 'bout
the size o' your'n."

"I think," said Annice, deciding not to ignore so broad a hint, "that I should be doing you no true kindness to give you such an article. A hat of mine would scarcely be a proper thing for you to wear."

"Well, now! do you think they ain't proper too?" asked Mrs. Shackles with an air of mingled surprise and relief. "Now I don't mind tellin' ye that I've al'ays thought them I've seen ye have on was kind o' flighty-tighty an' hardly respectable-like," she added confidentially. "But I didn't s'pose you thought so, an', thinks I, if a big city lady can stand 'em I s'pose I could — 'specially as I wouldn't have to go nowheres much to show it, only to the berry medders an' sich. I'd kiver it up mostly with a veil when I come in to sell berries — would if I had a veil, but I hain't got none an' don't know as I never will have. Can't you buy no other kind?" sympathizingly.

"You misunderstand me entirely," said Nan icily, but with a little red spot beginning to

burn on her cheeks. Her new pupil was hor-
ribly obtuse. "I mean that you and I are different persons — "

"Land sakes! Yes, I should hope so!" assented the old woman with uncomplimentary
fervor. "And the parson too — he's differenter
than either of us. Poor young boy! I wanted
to tell him, when he was a-preachin' away at
us folks to be contented with sich things as we
have, that all that was easy enough. It's bein'
contented with sich things as we haven't 's
where the pinch comes. Now I'm contented
with my new par'sol that Peggy Larrison jest
give me, but I ain't contented with my t'other
gown, 'cause I hain't got none. I'm 'bout your
size," reflectively, "only a little shorter and
broader — not so lean an' sprinky; but gowns
'll stretch awful, an' I don't mind runnin' a
tuck — "

"You need not explain. I do not propose
to give you one."

The lady's tone was losing dignity and

growing undeniably sharp. Mrs. Shackles squinted at her critically.

"Dear! Well, you needn't snap so; I ain't a-beggin'! 'Bout that parson o' your'n, I'll tell ye what he 'minds me of," she pursued, settling herself comfortably. "'Twas a circus I went to once. I don't go to 'em now, 'cause I don't have no money, an' there's no prospeck of nobody sendin' me a ticket; but 'twas real moril an' edifyin' — 'specially the clownd. I s'pose you go to every one that comes along, seein' you've nothin' to hender? I never seen but the one, an' I s'pose I wouldn't then, but me an' Humphrey wasn't long married, an' 'twas sort of our honeymoon — leastways our beeswax-moon, for there never was much honey to it, I'll be bound. Anyways we had a quarter, an' I went in bold as a lion, an' Humphrey he crep' under the canvas. He al'ays says his weddin' trip was a trip over them ropes that most broke his neck — an' 'twouldn't 'a' been no great loss neither, he's that shif'less.

But that clownd he jest went flyin' round. He was tryin' to help everybody, an' he'd run an' give this rope a little jerk an' then fly an' give that plank a little h'ist, al'ays managin' to take hold an' let go jest the wrong time, ye see, 'cause he was so took up with his own little performin' that he didn't rightly see what anybody else was tryin' to do or needin' to have done. 'Clare! I thought 'bout that circus right in the middle of the meetin' t'other night! 'Cause a body can keep awful busy an' help nobody, if they don't find out first where folks be an' what they're tryin' to do. Should think 'twas easy enough for folks to find out 'bout me, though, needin' shoes and bunnits, an' everything."

"Mrs. Shackles," said Annice severely — she was fully nerved to severity by this time — "it is a very poor and mistaken kindness for people to give you such things. It only encourages you to depend upon others instead of upon your own industry. You should be ashamed to do so.   You have no right to ask or expect other people to supply your wants. You should try to earn what you need, and to go without what you cannot earn.   That is the way to be respectable, if you are poor, and to be independent."

"La — sakes !"   There was a smouldering fire in the dim eyes as they surveyed the dainty silken-robed figure before them.   "Nobody oughtn't to have what they can't 'arn, eh ! What a sight o' work you must 'a' done to 'arn all them things you've got — silks, laces, dinners, carriages, fine houses, easy times — 'arned 'em all yourself!   An' your hands don't look like it neither."   She glanced from the smooth slender white fingers to her own hands, roughened, knotted and stained.   "I wish you'd tell me how you did it, 'cause I'd like to go into that business."

Truth is a pitiless weapon whatever hand wields it.   It suddenly occurred to Annice Lisle that there might be weak points in her

armor of virtuous superiority, or at least that uneducated eyes might fancy they detected such.

"It looks, if a body didn't know any better,
's if Humphrey might be in the same trade; but
he don't 'pear to prosper nigh so well — oh
my, no!" pursued the old woman. "Can't
you tell me what you've done an' how to do it?
If 'twouldn't be henderin' me from dependin'
on my own honest work, I'd like dreadful well
to know, 'cause you must have 'arned a good
deal in a short time. I don't mind tellin' ye
what I've done. I've picked berries in the
summer an' dug roots in the fall, an' I've
tramped miles through the sun an' rain to sell
'em. I've knit stockin's in winter, an' nussed
the sick when I could get a chance. I've
took care of a shif'less man an' buried all my
childern; an' if you think anybody's supported
me too much, I don't look as if they'd done it
extra sumptuous, for I ain't no beggar an' I
never will be. There's a good deal of nice-
soundin' talk 'bout stations an' sich, but the

short of it is that folks is folks, an' the biggest
ones on earth is nothin' but folks dressed up —
that's all. 'Arn all you get, to be sure!
There's them not a thousan' miles from here
would be satisfied if they could get all they
'arn. 'Tain't much use goin' round in shiny
broadcloth an' preachin' to 'em to be contented
with their lot — it's the lot some other folks is
gettin' they ain't contented with. Humph!" and
with a sniff indicative of other sentiments than
respect, Mrs. Shackles arose and departed.

Half way down the broad walk, she met
Miss Lyndal returning. The clouded old
brow cleared at her pleasant glance and
cheery good-morning.

"Well, you ain't one of the kind that thinks
you was made first an' the rest of the world
throwed in for fillin'!" she muttered.

"It is very enjoyable filling, such a morning
as this," Rachel laughed, without in the least
understanding the remark. "Have you walked
all the way from home so early?"

"Every step. Didn't seem so very early neither, with the sun blazin' down on a body; but Peggy Larrison she give me this par'sol. I come to bring home your scarf what I found in the road where 'twas dropped t'other night."

"Oh, you did? Thank you."

"An' I wanted to see you partic'lar to tell you 'bout one of them Baines babies bein' sick. They live in that old railroad car in the medder, you know."

"One of the twins? Poor Joe!" exclaimed Rachel, interested at once.

Mrs. Shackles looked gratified.

"I thought mebby you'd like to know, an' so I come"— she hesitated a moment, and the instinct or habit conquered her late resentment, and the memory of the homily she had just received, and she added —"so I come through the blazin', br'ilin' sun to tell you, though I hain't got no new apern to wear an' no prospeck of gettin' none."

"If you have taken so much trouble for me,

I think I must furnish you one," said Rachel, dropping a bit of silver in her hand.

"Rachel, how could you?" said her cousin indignantly, as she entered the room. " Actually thanking that impudent, begging old creature for making an errand here to bring back that scarf — entirely spoiled by a night in the rain — and when you know perfectly well that she expected to be paid for her coming ! "

" Well," answered Rachel serenely, " if Mr. Corry had found that scarf he would have brought it to me, and you would have been surprised if I had not thanked him in the politest manner possible. Why shouldn't I thank an old woman for the same doubtful service? And Mr. Corry would have expected recompense also — to the extent of a half-hour's chat and a few pieces of music. On the whole, I consider the quarter bestowed upon Mrs. Shackles cheaper and more satisfactory."

CHAPTER VI.

QUARRELLING WITH BREAD AND BUTTER.

A NOTE lay on Dr. Kelsey's office table — a tiny, innocent-looking note, and yet it evidently caused the doctor no little perturbation. He pondered its two or three lines as slowly and carefully as if the clear, legible sentences held something difficult to decipher or understand. Then he laid it slowly down and turned to the book he had been reading; but in a moment his eyes wandered and he took up the dainty bit of writing again. It was simple enough — a mere request that he would call upon a sick child in an old railroad car in the meadow — and signed "Rachel Lyndal." There was nothing more; the most intense gaze could evoke nothing beyond that brief business-like message. He pushed it aside once more and walked away to a distant window, but there was some magnetism about it that presently drew him back.

"And it ought to be no more to me than the most commonplace scrawl of a prescription — than any ill-spelled order left upon my office slate! Why should it be?" he muttered, pacing restlessly to and fro the length of the dingy room. "It is the wildest infatuation. Reason and common sense tell me that constantly and pitilessly enough, and yet —"

He looked about the sombre little office with its darkened walls, its faded carpet, the plain shelves that held his much-used books, and the table littered with papers and bearing traces of dust. His office boy was not particularly efficient, but neither did he charge an exorbitant price for his services, and the deficiencies in salary and dusting were expected to counterbalance each other — "with medical attendance for the boy's whole family furnished free," the doctor added when he made a mental summary of the matter. Certainly there was a marked contrast between this place and Judge Lyndal's office at the railway, or the beautiful rooms of his house. Dr. Kelsey had viewed such unimportant differences with philosophical serenity when he talked with Miss Lisle, but now, with the beautiful consistency of human nature, he smiled bitterly as he surveyed his small domain.

> "The skipper's jerkin ill beseems
> The lady's silken gown,"

he said. It was an unfortunate quotation, for instantly came those other words :

> " But love hath never known a law
> Beyond its own sweet will."

For a moment a sweet, earnest face seemed looking up at him from the paper. Then with a sternness that was almost fierceness, he turned away from the vision, denounced his own "unmitigated folly," and putting on his hat hurried into the street to escape from that haunting note and his own more haunting thoughts. Once in the open air, he turned his steps as rapidly in the direction of that car in the meadow as if no other patient in all the world had such need of or claim upon his services.

Yet the illness was not a serious one, he quietly informed Miss Lyndal when he met her on the street an hour later — merely a childish indisposition, a sudden cold and transient fever. In his determination to make it manifest that he understood the matter as she doubtless viewed it, a simple item of business, and in no way to be construed as any indication of friendship, he made his explanation of the case so coolly professional that it was rather overdone. The girl's fair face flushed as she passed on.

"How cool and odd he was! Exactly as if he were reading some article from a medical journal, instead of talking of a patient in whom he took a particle of interest. Perhaps he thought it silly to ask him to go there?" she mused with a blending of surprise and chagrin. Then she laughed. "Merely a childish indisposition, indeed! I fancy Joe considered it serious enough, — another case of 'nip and tuck,' probably."

Her slight resentment vanished, however, when she visited the car herself, and learned that the doctor had spent a half-hour there inquiring into every detail of the case, giving it his most careful attention, and doing all in his power for the little sufferer.

"I never did see a doctor so good," said Hitty gravely. "Tuck do be better, too, ma'am."

Mrs. Shackles was seated on one of the faded red-velvet cushions, and the small mistress of the mansion gratefully explained that she had stayed with them a part of the previous night.

"Ought to know how to take keer of childern after havin' buried all my own," said Mrs. Shackles, as cheerfully as if that consumma-

tion were all that could be desired, and proved
possession of the highest skill.

"An' she brought 'em some milk," pursued
Hitty in her sober, pleased way.

That was what she had done with the milk
begged the day before! Miss Lisle would
have been doubly disgusted had she heard the
old woman's brisk reply.

"Land sakes! I didn't want it. Leastways"
— suddenly remembering where and how she
had obtained it — "it ain't good for folks to
drink when they've been trampin' through the
hot sun an' hain't got no peppermint to take
after it, an' no prospeck of gettin' none. Humphrey he says to me, 'Why don't we have such
things?' an' I says to him, 'Why don't we keep
a drug-store, or a fam'ly carriage?'"

"We'll have carriages," quavered old Simon,
suddenly aroused by the word, "horses an'
velvety carriages, when the prize comes to-
morrer — or next week. D'ye think it'll mebby
be to-morrer, Hitty?"

"Not 'fore next week, Daddy," said Hitty soothingly.

"An' next week I'll have a new fiddle with diamonds on it, an' we'll have clo'es an' houses an' pianers — pianers — Hitty!" impatiently, "Why can't ye tell the lady we'll be grand folks ourselves next week? Pianers an' — what?"

"Sofys an' carpets an' mebby gold dishes, Daddy," enumerated Hitty. Then she lifted her appealing eyes to Rachel. "I'm sure Tuck does be better to-day, ma'am?"

"Dr. Kelsey said he would soon be well again," Rachel answered re-assuringly. She was about to inquire for Joe, but Mrs. Shackles had taken up old Simon's words.

"Houses an' diamonds? Land sakes! If you've got any prospeck of all them things you're better off 'n most poor folks, I can tell ye! There's lots of 'em round here that hain't got no prospeck of nothin' but trouble — the men out o' work, an' worse a-threat'nin'. It's very fine for the bosses at the shops to put off the blasts, or whatsumever they call it, a leetle later an' a leetle later, an' so get hours of extra work crowded in; but when the men sets up agin it, they're quarrellin' with their bread an' butter, bless ye! They're that igernant an' blind that they're al'ays a-quarrellin' with their bread an' butter. If they knowed more 'bout communion an' the Frinch revolution they wouldn't do it, but they has such peaceful times, poor folks does, that their bread an' butter is mostly all they can quarrel with — though there's so little of it that a body wouldn't think there'd be much of a fight neither. So them men's out o' work."

The old woman was apparently talking to no one but herself. Hitty heard without in the least comprehending — she understood very few of Mrs. Shackles' rambling discourses. Rachel's attention was seemingly absorbed in watching the flushed face of the little sleeper, but she was startled. Was there

any new trouble? Had Mrs. Shackles any
purpose of telling her something which she
suspected she did not know, with a thought
that she might possibly possess power to help?
A faint smile crossed her lips, its sadness
tinged with bitterness. She glanced down at
the slender hands resting on the back of the
old car-seat where the little one lay.

"As helpless as any other girl's hands.
They may wear more costly rings because
they belong to Judge Lyndal's daughter,
but that is the only way in which they can
have any connection with the affairs of the
road," she thought. If with that consciousness
she could but wash them of all responsiblity
"before the multitude," or before her own
troubled soul! — but she could not.

Mrs. Shackles had found a new theme, and
was discoursing to Simon of the best time and
place for digging sassafras root, though he
assured her, with a complacent chuckle, that
he should " have to dig for nothin' much longer

—not longer 'n next week." It was probable
she had meant nothing beyond the pleasure of
hearing herself talk, for her voice was still
running steadily on as Rachel walked slowly
away down the meadow path where the clover-
heads were nodding. The fragrance and the
quietness lured her on, and it was by a long
and circuitous route that she reached home
as the last slant beams of the afternoon sun
were fading from the piazza. From the room
beyond came a little ripple of music, faint and
cool like the tinkle of a fountain, and then a
murmur of conversation. Nan had been playing, and her fingers still wandered occasionally
over the keys as she talked—a fashion of
hers. Heman and Mr. Corry were there, and
Rachel would have passed on but for her
cousin's quick arresting voice.

"Oh, my dear," with that peculiar intonation
by which Miss Lisle contrived to express surprise, a hint of violated proprieties and a general mingling of toleration and disapproval,

"don't vanish again.' One must capture you on the wing if they would have you at all, you are such a bird of long flights. We were just talking of a visit to the railroad shops. It is a long time since I have been through them, and Heman, for some reason, has never inspected them."

"For a number of reasons," corrected that gentleman meditatively. His visits to Craig's Cross had been fewer than Miss Lisle's, and they occurred always in summer when the shops had only suggested themselves to him as hot, dirty and exceedingly uncomfortable places of resort. Had he heard any call of duty in their direction he would not have shunned them; he was neither cowardly nor insincere, but as a pleasure they were extremely doubtful. However, that was not an opinion to be expressed if the ladies cared to go. "It is a pity they are not running at night," pursued Miss Lisle. "They would lose their commonplace aspect then, and become more weird and impressive — the foundry particularly."

"The foundry is not running at all," said Mr. Corry. He had rolled forward a chair for Rachel, and was busied in disengaging a curtain against which he had inadvertently placed it. "At least it is not doing its regular work, I am sorry to say on your account."

He spoke carelessly, as if there could be no other cause for regret; and as Dr. Kelsey, coming down from Mrs. Lyndal's room, joined them for a moment, he turned at once to him. If he had hoped to change the conversation he was disappointed.

"Is it not an unusual time for stopping?" questioned Mr. Weldon after a minute's pondering. "I should have supposed it to be your busiest season."

"Not exactly that. Still we had no intention of stopping; the men are responsible for it, not we." Mr. Corry's laugh had a touch of embarrassment. "The moulders are favoring

us with that senseless and rather annoying per-
formance, a strike; but the other shops are
working as usual, Miss Lisle, and the wood-
work and painting departments are, to my
mind, much better worth visiting. It is disinterested of me to say that, too, since the foundry is more especially in my province."

"How long since this happened?" Rachel
asked.

"Since the foundrymen stopped? Two or
three weeks."

"And what reason did they give?"

What a way the girl had of inquiring into
such matters as if they particularly interested
her! Why could she not call the affair
"shocking" or "provoking," or designate it by
some other feminine adjective and dismiss it,
as another girl would have done? But her
gray eyes were as steady and grave as if she
were called upon to decide where the right
and wrong of the controversy lay, instead of
taking it for granted, as Judge Lyndal's daugh-

ter might have been expected to do. It occurred to Mr. Corry that it might sometimes be
inconvenient to be closely related to a woman,
however charming, who insisted upon asking
such questions.   Then he smiled as he reflected that probably she did not ask her father.

"There was some dissatisfaction about irregular hours, I believe.   They complained that
the heats were made so late that they were
compelled to work over-hours ; and then there
was a reduction in wages, and they rebelled
against that.   They couldn't have everything
they wanted, and so they wisely determined
to have nothing, and stopped work altogether,"
Mr. Corry explained, since it seemed impossible to avoid talking "shop."

"And the reductions were necessary, I suppose?"

The question was asked wistfully, but the
gentleman smiled at its innocent ignorance.

"Oh, well, times are hard, you know, and
there are reductions everywhere.   We are

only following the general order. You ladies don't understand much about such things in your 'silken bowers.'" He looked admiringly around the pretty room and laughed.

"We ought at least to understand enough to know whether we have any right to the silken bowers," she said slowly.

He did not comprehend, perhaps did not hear the remark, but added, —

"They had not sense enough to consult their own interest by making the best of what could not be helped. They are a foolish, obstinate set of fellows, ready to spend a dollar to save fifty cents at any time. So they grumbled and protested, and finally struck. It is no general movement through the shops, but only among the foundrymen. They belong to a trades' union, of course."

"That whole system of unions is a great evil," said Heman reflectively. "There ought to be some means of eradicating it."

Dr. Kelsey laughed.

"Its root is wide-spreading, Mr. Weldon. We physicians divide ourselves into allopathic, homœopathic, &c., and bar each other out from our societies, and refuse to practise together. You ministers, in your different sects, do the same; and I do not know why the trades should not have equal rights with the professions in that line."

"But that is a very different thing — entirely different. Why, those trades' unions are dreadful!" said Annice decidedly. "Did you ever read 'Put Yourself in His Place'? They commit such horrible deeds!"

"Oh, we have nothing of that sort to contend with," Mr. Corry admitted frankly. "As much as I dislike the organizations in this country, I will do them the justice to confess that I do not believe they either counsel or countenance such proceedings. The deeds of violence we hear of in such connections are usually the acts of irresponsible individuals, or they occur among foreigners — the lowest and most ignorant of them. Americans, as most of our skilled workmen are, do not take kindly to murdering and incendiarism. Societies, constitutions, laws, and a general fusillade about rights and liberties, suit the national disposition, however, and I must own they find ways of being troublesome enough without firearms or bludgeons. They have actually prevented our hiring other men in their places, by hanging around the stations, watching trains, talking to all we have brought here, and by persuasion, bribery and their whole representation of the case, have either coaxed or frightened nearly every one away. Besides, a majority of the best workmen, such as we really want, belong to the union, and they, of course, will not come."

"And meanwhile how are these men supporting their families?" asked Annice. "How silly of them to waste time and money in such petty vengeance! If they are not willing to work for what you offer, why not leave the place to others, and go away and find work elsewhere?"

"That last is not so easily done." There was a perceptible note of triumph in Mr. Corry's calm voice, and he smiled. "We have taken the liberty of notifying manufacturers in the city and in towns near by, that they will confer a favor upon us by not employing our insubordinate workmen. And a company like ours is not without influence, Miss Lisle. These very independent foundrymen have been refused when they applied for places, and they will probably be wiser if not happier before they reach the end of this little scheme which they were so anxious to inaugurate."

Rachel's lips were suddenly compressed.

"Did you say that the railroad company had done this?" she asked.

" Not formally, as a company, of course; it was scarcely worth that," he answered carelessly. "The superintendent of the foundry, and some of us connected in one way or another with that department; but it had the same weight."

There was a faint sigh of relief at the answer, but Mr. Corry did not notice it. He had not intended to speak of the matter. It scarcely suited his ideas of a topic for the drawing-room, but since the interest of his hearers had fairly launched him upon it, he was not unwilling to explain it fully.

"Moreover, since they were so exceedingly particular about their rights and laws," he continued, "we propose to see that they are not defrauded of their rights under a certain law passed by our State legislature. It provides that persons combining together to injure the property or business of others, as they have done, shall be guilty of conspiracy and subject to the penalty of a heavy fine or a term of imprisonment in the penitentiary. We intend the ringleaders in the movement shall have the full benefit of that latter clause."

There was a moment's silence.

"That seems pretty severe, under the circumstances, doesn't it?" Mr. Weldon remarked doubtfully.

"At first thought, perhaps; but severity to the few is often kindness to the many, you know, and these fellows need above all things to learn prudence and common sense. The idea of one of the shops being closed for two or three weeks because their demands are not listened to! A good sharp lesson that will teach them not to quarrel with their bread and butter, and not to interfere with that of other people, will really be a blessing to them, however they learn it;" and Mr. Corry smiled again — a smile that did not soften his handsome face, but only showed its determined lines, and glittered for an instant in the steel-blue eyes. "I fancy they are already somewhat uneasy. They have consulted a lawyer, I understand. But the facts can be proven beyond all possibility of denial, and I do not see how he can by any means save them from the full penalty of the law."

He picked up Rachel's fan which had fallen to the floor, but she shrank involuntarily from contact with the hand which restored it — a white shapely hand, comely enough if one were not in its grasp — and her murmured word of acknowledgment was scarcely audible. There was an uncomfortable pause in the conversation. Then Dr. Kelsey delivered a message he had brought from Mrs. Lyndal, and turned away. But Rachel, abruptly rising, accompanied him to the hall. Something in her face made him linger a moment.

"I know about these people, I know their homes," she said, without preface or explanation.

He bowed. "I know them also."

"They are not criminals, Dr. Kelsey. If the company had a right to decide what they would pay, surely the men had a right to choose whether they would accept or refuse the terms offered them; and if they were wrong in preventing others from taking the places they left, was it not at least an equal wrong which barred the way to their obtaining employment elsewhere? They have been honest, industrious, useful workers. They do not belong to the class that must be imprisoned for the good of society, — they are no criminals."

"There is crime enough in the affair somewhere, but I do not agree with Mr. Corry in selection of the ringleaders," said the doctor with grim quietness.

"I know about their homes," Rachel repeated as if that one thought haunted her — "plain, cheerful, cosey little homes, dependent for all their brightness and comfort upon the wages of the one worker, but honest and respectable as any in the land. There are gentle, true-hearted women in them, and sweet little children, whom this sorrow and shame will crush and kill. And these men are guilty of no crime — at least it seems so to me — that their families should be left helpless and disgraced, and they themselves imprisoned with the most degraded and vicious."

"Mr. Corry says they are foolish, obstinate and troublesome—" Dr. Kelsey closed his lips as if his sentence were not ended, but suppressed. It might be better to leave his whole thought unspoken unless he had opportunity to express it to the gentleman himself.

"Dr. Kelsey, I must know about this—whether anything can be done," she said with voice growing a little unsteady. "Will you inquire for me? Find what lawyer they have engaged, these men, and learn from him? If there should be help needed, anything I can furnish—it sounds strangely for me to say it, but I will do it!" There was a sudden flash in the gray eyes.

"I understand." The doctor's voice was calm and re-assuring, as if her confidence were the most ordinary and natural thing in the world. "I can easily learn all about it. I will find exactly how the case stands, and let you know."

"Thank you."

She extended her hand. It was a trembling little hand, just then, seeking strength and support somewhere, and it rested unconsciously in his for a moment. For a moment he looked down upon it as if sorely tempted to claim it for a longer, closer holding; then he bade her a grave good-by and left her.

"Grandmamma's prescriptions must require minute and explicit directions, and much re-iteration!" commented Nan with an arch laugh that scarcely glossed the impertinence of the remark.

Even quiet Rachel could be haughty upon rare occasions. She vouchsafed neither smile nor word of reply, but bestowed upon her cousin a cool inquiring glance which sent that young lady to turning over the contents of a music portfolio, and inspired Heman to remark upon some recent discoveries in Herculaneum. Buried cities were at least safe. But while they talked of exhumations and inscriptions, some words from an ancient book were running sadly through Rachel's thought :

"And on the side of their oppressors there was power : but they had no comforter."

CHAPTER VII.

IN THE SAME BOAT.

DR. KELSEY journeyed cityward, two or
three days later, in pursuit of drugs and
information. For the former he could have
sent or could have waited, but he could brook
no delay in regard to the latter, nor could he
trust another. He had learned that the foundrymen, wisely divining that their chance for
skilful counsel and strong legal support would
be greater outside of Craig's Cross, where the
influence and power of the railroad company
were all-pervasive, had sought aid in the city.
He had obtained the name of the firm and
determined upon an interview.

"Yes, sir, y-e-s," answered the gray-haired,
keen-eyed gentleman to whom he presently
introduced himself and his mission; "I think

we have a little matter of that kind on nand;
I recollect it."

Dr. Kelsey did not doubt that he recollected
clearly, even though the handsomely appoint-
ed office, the mighty array of books and
papers, and the unconcerned air of the legal
gentleman, seemed to imply that the imprisonment or release of a few workmen, or of a
few railroad corporations, or of two thirds of
the human family indeed, would be a trifling
incident soon banished from the judicial mind
by more weighty concerns.

What did he think of the case? That it was
not easy to discover — certainly not until he
had found out what he thought of his visitor;
and perceiving this, Dr. Kelsey allowed him
to take silent and conversational observations,
and facilitated them by explaining, as frankly
as it was possible to do, the ground of his
interest. The lawyer's face slowly cleared.
He laughed.

"You came from Craig's Cross, you see, and

I understand the road pretty nearly own that place, buildings and people, souls and bodies, so I did not know what connection you might have with the matter. Yes, sir, the case has been placed in our hands."

"And what are the chances for the men, if I may ask?"

"Chances? We-ll," the lawyer smiled again; "the law seems to be explicit enough — and I suppose there is no doubt of its infringement in this case. There may be some adjustment, possibly, or compromise. I have solicited an interview in that direction."

He spoke slowly, his elbows resting on the arms of his chair, the finger-tips of the right hand matching themselves carefully against those of the left, as if he were putting together the pieces of a puzzle. There was a slight sound at the outer door, and the gentleman raised his head; the air of deliberation suddenly changed to alertness and decision. He glanced at his watch.

"Pardon me, I have an appointment. No, do not go," as his visitor made a movement toward departure. "If you are at leisure, please remain a few minutes, and I will see you again. I shall not be long occupied, and I may be able to answer your inquiries more definitely."

A wave of his hand seemed to place the apartment in the doctor's possession, and that gentleman, who had begun to despair of obtaining any information, decided to comply with the suggestion and wait a little longer. As he resumed his seat the lawyer vanished into the adjoining office, leaving, either accidentally or designedly, the door between the two rooms ajar. Dr. Kelsey took up a daily paper, one of the articles the waving hand had apparently placed at his disposal, and for a minute or two was only absently conscious of the occupants or conversation of the next room. Some one had entered, and they were talking. It was nothing that interested him, of course, beyond a passing reflection that if the new-comer paid for a legal opinion it was to be hoped he might obtain something worthy of being called one.

Then his indifference was effectually banished by a voice familiar and unmistakable which reached him clearly.

"I came merely to avoid the discourtesy of refusing your request, though I regard it as a useless one. I see no necessity for discussing the matter until it is presented in all its bearings, and in proper form, before the court," said Mr. Stephen Corry.

"Let me hope you will not regret coming, nevertheless," replied the lawyer's low bland tones. He had placed chairs by a small table in the centre of the room, where the remainder of the conversation was unavoidably audible to the inmate of the adjoining room. "We may agree upon some plan of adjustment that will obviate the necessity of a trial. We may be able to arrange some terms —"

"We do not wish to make any," interposed Mr. Corry decidedly.

" Ah? We-ll, but courts are large bodies that move slowly, you know, and their decisions cannot always be certainly determined—"

"We are content that they shall move slowly, but we expect in this case that they will move very surely," interrupted Mr. Corry again.

The eyes under the lawyer's bushy gray brows noted the triumph in his face.

" The laws as administered by our courts are, of necessity, rigid," pursued the attorney, tapping with a pencil the green baize of the table. " They cannot be made flexible enough to accommodate themselves to all the varying circumstances. In this case, now, it is probable these men did not know of the existence of a law so defining conspiracy?"

" I presume not," Mr. Corry smiled grimly. " People should be wise enough to look before they leap, however. It would have been the part of common sense to discover whether their undertaking was a lawful one before they entered upon it."

The lawyer's answering smile was a peculiar one.

"Many who claim to be far wiser than they fall into that error, Mr. Corry."

"Possibly." Mr. Corry was not interested in the frailties of humanity in general. "One thing these fellows did know, however — that they were injuring us by preventing our hiring others in their stead. They fully intended that."

"But if that annoyance should cease?" the attorney suggested.

"It assuredly will cease with the perpetrators safely behind prison bars. That will be the best guarantee in the world," insisted the younger man's hard triumphant tones. "Besides, they will have ample opportunity to meditate upon the laws of the land, and improve upon their ignorance. The improvement of the condition of the working classes is a question that is greatly agitating the reformers, you know. We will contribute our mite towards its solution."

"Ye-s. You think these men should have submitted quietly to the reduction of wages?"

"It would have been far more sensible than any other course; but if they did not choose that, they should not have attempted to prevent our hiring others. We intend they shall have cause to repent of that proceeding."

"I should have supposed you held the means of retaliation in your own hands. Could you not induce other shops and foundries not to employ them? Give them a taste of the same medicine, eh?"

"We attended to that very effectually," said Mr. Corry with his scornful smile once more. "They have had the benefit of an experience in that direction that they will be likely to remember, I fancy. They have at least learned that our influence is potent in many quarters."

"Ah!" The keen eyes closed for a moment in apparent meditation. "And now you wish to add a legal prosecution? But these men, so far as I can learn, are not dangerous members of society, not of the depraved and vicious class at all? And the penitentiary is an ugly place to send a man, Mr. Corry — an ugly place. Then there are the families to be considered."

"They should have considered them," said Mr. Corry shortly; "it is their business, not ours. Besides, they are not doing much for their families while they are hanging around out of work. But the long and short of the subject is, that we intend these men and all others shall be taught, once for all, that our company, its shops, rules, and whole plans of working, are to be respected and let alone; that they cannot be trifled with, interfered with, or fought against safely. A sentence of imprisonment, which we fully intend these fellows shall have if we can secure it, — and of that we have little doubt, — will at least be a salutary warning to others. I may as well tell you at once that you are wasting time in this interview. You are acting in the interest of these men, I understand, but we will not quash the case by any compromise or agreement."

"We-ll, I had none to propose," said the lawyer slowly. "I was merely asking you to view it in all its aspects. I think you are correct about the law. If you prosecute you can get the men convicted; I do not mind giving that as my opinion. It is probable you can procure them a term in the penitentiary — I do not see how it can be helped. But," the slow speculative manner suddenly vanished, and the keen eyes flashed a fiery glance upon the astonished face opposite them, "as surely as you do it, sir, you shall go with them!"

"I —what do you mean?" demanded Mr. Corry, surprised even beyond anger for the moment.

"I mean exactly what I say, sir. You to talk of 'looking before leaping,' and the duty of making sure an act is no infringement of law before committing it, indeed! You did not even see that you had done precisely what they did! If they conspired to prevent your obtaining workmen, you employers also conspired to prevent their obtaining work elsewhere, and so successfully, by your own showing, as to do them great injury. The law covers the one action as completely as the other, and if you choose to prosecute under it, you shall share whatever measure you mete to others — be assured of that! Do you see?"

Mr. Corry did see. He muttered something about "threats and bravado," but he did not complete the sentence. He was wise enough to understand that he had blundered. The lawyer opened a heavily bound volume and laid it before him.

"There is the law, sir. You will see that, very stupidly, it cuts both ways."   .

Mr. Corry read it in silence; he seemed disposed to remain silent.

"As I said before," pursued the attorney, calmly, "with proper persistence and management, you can steer that obnoxious crew into the penitentiary, but you, with two or three other gentlemen of your corporation, are in the same boat — that is all."

Mr Corry arose stiffly.

"It would be folly to pretend that I do not understand you, or that—" His face was at white heat, but he held his voice and words in check. "Of course this ends the matter—for *this time,*" with savage emphasis on the last two words; "but I advise you to warn your clients that all interference with our employment of men must cease."

"Ah! Thank you for reminding me of that point! About your opposition to their obtaining work elsewhere — I presume you will withdraw all that? Notify those manufacturers that your objections to the employment of these men have ceased, or something of that sort? I advise you to nullify, as speedily as possible, any such notices you may have sent out. Such writings prove ugly documents occasionally, Mr. Corry, very ugly. Good-morning, sir."

If Mr. Corry replied, the words were lost in the sharp closing of the door as he departed. The lawyer whistled softly and rubbed his hands together.   Then he walked back into the office where Dr. Kelsey awaited him.

"You heard?" he questioned with a smile.

"I heard.   Thank you for-allowing me the privilege."

"And are you satisfied?"

"Perfectly satisfied," laughed the doctor.

"We-ll," the lawyer relapsed into his meditative air, "it is strange how blindly people will persist in setting traps for others exactly in their own path."

"You think Mr. Corry and the others will recall their opposition to the employment of the men elsewhere, as you suggested?"

"Undoubtedly."   The word was slow and emphatic, and a smile twinkled under the bushy eyebrows.   "Probably they will compromise in some way and re-employ some of the men themselves, though for a time the civilities between the two parties will be as punctilious, and their love for each other as great, as that of two duellists who are watching for a chance to shoot each other; but they will each have learned something of the other's marksmanship."

Comfortably settling himself in a railway carriage that afternoon, for his homeward journey, Dr. Kelsey unexpectedly encountered Mr. Corry as a seat-mate. He had not recognized the curled-up figure, with hat drawn low over the face, in time, or he would have avoided a meeting, for that gentleman was evidently not in his most genial humor. Usually his manners and language were unexceptionable, but when he remarked upon the disagreeable day, with a forcible adjective, and explained that he had a headache — also with an adjective — as a reason for drawing his hat down again and making no further attempts at conversation, the doctor gladly excused him from further effort.

He had quite regained his equanimity when they chanced to meet again, several days later, at Judge Lyndal's.

"By the way, our shops are all running again," he announced carelessly to Miss Lisle. "I mention it that you ladies may know we are ready for a visit, if you are disposed so to honor us. Perhaps Miss Rachel knew already?" with a quick glance.

Miss Rachel did not commit herself.

"You have supplied the vacant places, then?" she questioned.

"Oh, yes."

"And what has become of those other men who were so troublesome?" asked Annice Lisle.

"Why — we re-employed some of them. In fact we thought it better, under the circumstances, to effect a compromise," explained Mr. Corry graciously. "They are fair workmen — we had nothing to complain of in that line — and they are ignorant, you know, and probably did not understand the full scope of the law they were breaking. They need work, and they have families. In short, we thought it wise to yield a little."

"It was very kind," said Nan admiringly. "I hope they will at least be grateful."

Rachel and the doctor exchanged a swift significant glance — a delicious bit of confidence that made Dr. Kelsey's heart throb. He assured himself, as he rode away, that it was a mere happening, and that his feeling concerning it was absurd. Nevertheless, he felt the thrill to his finger-tips whenever he remembered the glance of those dark-gray eyes, and it consoled him under the disapproval of one of his most persistent patients, who dated an entirely new ache from "that day when you went off so unexpectedly to the city, upon a pressing errand — I hope it was a pressing errand that took you from your duty, Doctor — and neglected to call."

CHAPTER VIII.

A TALE UNTOLD.

DR. KELSEY'S patients were favored with flowers that season. The happening of a single morning grew, no one quite knew why or how, into an established custom, and the luxuriant old garden on the hillside sent its choice treasures of bloom to narrow little homes in the town below whenever the doctor could be the messenger. And as Mrs. Lyndal's venerable medical adviser was fast dropping much of his practice into his junior's hands, and as Mrs. Lyndal graciously acquiesced in the change, the elder physician's visits grew rare and Dr. Kelsey's more frequent.

So, through many mornings, clusters of dewy blossoms awaited him in the spacious hall — given him by Rachel, or, if she by chance were absent, placed ready for his finding. Annice Lisle began to question whether, entertaining such romantic fancies, he could be sufficiently practical for his profession. Yet nothing could have been more matter-of-fact than the manner in which these floral donations were waited for and received, or the tone in which the occasionally added request was preferred — " A stray blossom for the carrier, Miss Lyndal?"

These last — rosebud, pansy or spray of dainty whitebells, as Rachel's passing fancy suggested — he placed in his button-hole " as carelessly," Nan averred, " as he would cram vials or powders in his pocket." And if, when out on the quiet hillside road, they received more attentive glances, brushed across a moustached lip, and were replaced and guarded with jealous care, they never returned to tell the story — foolish story at which the doctor himself muttered " Folly ! "

The weeks, slipping by, sent Heman back to his studies again, and Nan once more to her city home. The garden lost its glories, but the trees, in compensation, hung out their gayest colors. Mrs. Shackles had changed the contents of her basket from the latest berries to roots and herbs, and finally, as the frosts increased, to nuts.

"An' now it's comin' 'most time when there ain't one airthly thing to gather unless folks would buy snowballs ; an' I hain't saved nigh enough to buy a warm shawl yet, an' I need one," she complained. "It's goin' to be a dreadful hard winter ! "

Rachel heard that last sentence, repeated in various forms, from many different sources as she talked here and there with the odd acquaintances of her rambles, or saw, as she did more and more of late, those who on different errands sought her father at the house. It was growing to be her share of the road, in those days, to meet and know of the troubled anxious ones whom she could not help, and to feel a sense of guilt in the sharp contrast of her own sheltered, abundant life.

"Do not try to carry the weight of all the world's woes, Miss Lyndal," laughed Dr. Kelsey meeting her in the hall one day; "it is too heavy a load." Then, noticing and trying to read her clouded face, he added more gravely, "One only can do that — has done it. However things seem to go, 'the King never dies.'"

She smiled, and caught the comforting of the thought. But she could not tell him of that vague but painful sense of responsibility that rested upon her — the feeling of guilt, not her own, but another's, that often weighed so oppressively and made the luxuries lavished upon her seem almost the fruits of robbery. A strange humility was creeping over the girl in the presence of those whom she often met — those to whom the winter had indeed grown hard. She knew that scant wages had been still further reduced, and that their tardy payment lessened them yet more. Meanwhile the treasurer's beautiful house was completed, — whoever had furnished foundations or walls, — and her father had hundreds of dollars to spare for his many plans and schemes. There was a wrong somewhere. She could not untangle the vexed question and read it plainly; but the pain and doubt of it haunted her, and brought sometimes the thought that she would willingly exchange lots with some of those in the little homes along the line, if so she could feel free from stain and thoroughly honest. Only a girl's morbid fancies? Assuredly her father would have said so had her thoughts been open to his inspection. Even her occasional questions and remarks aroused him one day to an unusually critical scrutiny of her face, and a suggestion that she needed change and something to amuse her — a regret that she had not returned to the city with Nan, and then a sudden conclusion : " I suppose you are puzzling your head

with some of Heman's impracticable ministe-
rial nonsense."

The utter injustice of that remark provoked
a smile. Heman might indeed pray, "Give us
this day our daily bread," as he had always
been taught, but it would certainly never
have occurred to him to add, "And keep us
from trying to take away that of other people."

The Judge loved his daughter — after his
fashion, and when he had leisure. He mentally decided that all girls liked company and
gayety, of course, and another winter something different from life in that quiet old place
must be planned for her; and then he straight-
way forgot the matter in interests more absorb-
ing.

But Rachel was content to be in her home.
Hers was a healthful nature, however her
generous heart and honest soul were wounded
by their surroundings. She needed neither
excitement nor constant companionship. River,
hillside and wood, in their glittering winter

beauty, suited her; and though Dr. Kelsey frequently met her in the dwellings of some of his patients, — drawn there not alone by kindness and sympathy, but by that vague sense of some reparation due, — he saw her often elsewhere, in the long rides and rambles that now, as in her childhood, were her delight.

Those chance meetings, the passing salutations, the short rides or walks together, the brief interviews in her home and elsewhere, — grown longer of late, though they still seemed so brief, — were more to Rachel than she knew. At least she did not analyze their pleasantness. She only realized that the presence of this strong, honest manhood made her world nobler and better; that the blithe, cheery manner, though it could soften to tenderness when needful, held for her the healthful freshness of a sea-breeze. His straightforward earnestness that pierced through shams to the underlying truth, drew, irresistibly, her confidence ; and the consciousness of his friendship was growing more and more — she did not know or question why — into a thought of hopefulness and strength. There was, too, a scarcely recognized feeling that if the doubts and questions that troubled her should grow too heavy to be borne alone, she could rely upon his ready comprehension, truth and help.

To the doctor the subject stood in clearer light. He pondered it often, pacing up and down his office, or staring dreamily into the fire, when an earnest face with its frame of bright hair had looked up at him from the printed pages of heavy books, and obscured dry treatises on tissues and molecules.

Seeing her, day after day, in her simple, girlish grace, learning the charm of her pure thoughtful womanliness, watching, as they talked together, the deepening and brightening of the gray eyes that read and answered his thoughts so swiftly, it seemed only natural to love her — nay, impossible to do otherwise. Then he felt that she belonged to him as to no other, and sure of his power and right to win her. But there were other hours, away from her, in his office or on lonely rides, when he remembered the wealth in which her life was cradled, and the position and surroundings that might be hers at will. He assured himself then that he had but mistaken her frank friendship; that his love for her was folly, madness. Their paths were wholly unlike, and must lie forever apart.

The latter mood held the other in abeyance, and guarded look and tone. He had no right to lure her, if indeed he could, to a lot that even to himself looked rugged and hard in contrast with her own. True it held the sweetness of honest usefulness.

"But that she cannot miss. A life like hers is in itself a blessing," he murmured, watching her.

The old battle had fought itself over, one

wintry day, until, weary of it and himself, he
abandoned unsuccessful attempts to study or
write, and forsook his office. Swift movement
through the cold air would cool his brain and
suit his mood, he fancied, and he sought the
river, skates in hand. A goodly number of
skaters were there before him, enjoying what
might prove the last sport of the season, for
the ice was already broken in the middle of the
river, though a wide smooth border stretched
out from the shores.

It was a pretty sight — the blocks of ice
piled upon the bank, the clear track and the
flying forms. His quick eye recognized at
once one slender, gray-robed figure, brightened
by dashes of crimson in cap and trimmings, as,
a little apart from its companions, it glided
away on its course. The motion suited her,
he thought. Separate from all others she
always seemed to him. He watched, but did
not join her. She had not seen him, and he
would not seek her, so he went on his own

swift way with compressed lips and resolute eyes that scarcely told of pleasure-seeking.

He shunned companionship as far as possible, exchanging only brief greetings with those whom he met, and skated away where others were not. The river looked dreary in its iciness, that day, and the hills, between which it lay, wore an air of desolateness with their gaunt leafless trees and patches of sharp rocks. The western range flung long shadows, but the eastern caught gleams of red gold from the late afternoon sunshine.

Up and down the long smooth course the doctor passed — now away alone, then returning for a glimpse of one slender, graceful skater. He was not used to indulging moods and reveries, but he gave them uncontrollable freedom then, and let fancy whisper gloomily that his life must be like this hard, cold track, shut in by barren rugged walls of duty.

Suddenly a commotion arose among the skaters further out. There were shouts and cries, a confused mingling of voices, and hurrying to and fro, that attracted even Dr. Kelsey's attention. A murmur of—"Broken away!"—a sharp call, "Oh, be quick!" drew his wandering eyes. A mass of ice had parted from the main body, and was floating out with several persons upon it. One quick glance revealed among them a figure in gray and crimson; and, pausing for no second glance, he turned in his course and sped rapidly towards it.

The floe was already separated from the solid ice by a narrow chasm of dark water. Several leaped across it towards the shore while the doctor was making his way to the place, but a chorus of halloos, startled and questioning, greeted him as, with one swift bound, he cleared the black, widening line in an opposite direction. Neither heeding nor hearing, he swept on towards Rachel, who, after a moment, recognizing, advanced to meet him. She hardly comprehended until then what had happened.

"Come! quick!" he uttered hoarsely, breathless from the effort he had made, but hurrying her forward while the steel upon his own feet seemed still to hold the swiftness of wings.

But it was in vain. Reaching once more the dividing chasm, a single look showed that the feat which had before been difficult was now impossible. The rapidly widening stream forbade all hope of crossing. Others who had also been at the further side of the loosened mass came flying to the verge, and paused in dire dismay as they realized that the chance of escape was gone. Five in all remained as occupants of the treacherous floating island.

For a moment or two there was a rapid interchange of shouts — useless directions, fruitless appeals or words of encouragement. Then, following each other slowly, the party at last all retreated from the more dangerous margin to the centre of the floe. Rachel looked up at her companion with white face, but with steady eyes still.

" There is nothing to be done — nothing that we can do," he said, answering their questioning. " We must wait for others."

On the shore the groups were already scattering, clambering up the bank, and flying hither and thither to spread the alarm and bring assistance ; though what successful plan of help or rescue could be devised it was difficult to foresee. But, with that little trembling hand on his arm, Horace Kelsey felt that for him the situation, in all its peril, held compensating sweetness. Yet he with difficulty repressed the words that sprang to his lips, and only strove to uphold her courage with what hope he could offer.

" I do not understand how you are here," she said wonderingly, a little later, when the first shock and bewilderment of their situation had so far passed as to leave room for surprise at any details. " I did not know you were on the ice. Surely you could not have been on this part of it ? "

"Not until a few minutes ago. I saw you, and was coming to join you."

He did not tell her that he came only when he saw her in danger.

"You could have escaped if you had not stopped for me," she said, without surmising the whole truth. After a moment she added in a lower tone, "We are in great peril, I suppose, — I know it must be so; and yet we are in health and strength, and the sweet, every-day life so close to us, — I cannot realize that death is near."

"And life is very sweet to you?"

It was not wholly an interrogation, but she looked up questioningly. Yet when she had replied she had substituted another word for his.

"Yes, life is — precious."

Why should it not be, with all that belonged to hers? For his own — But earth's sharp contrasts grew strangely dim in an hour like this, and he remembered remorsefully the dreary pictures of his own lot he had drawn but a

little while before. With all its work, its hope,
its duty, the love of dear ones in that little
home far away, — its possibilities of usefulness,
even if it held no brighter possession, — how
had he dared to call it barren and hard?

The sun dropped lower behind the hills, — a
great red ball that seemed to give out no
warmth, — and sank out of sight, while the
radiance slowly vanished from the eastern hill-
tops. The party gathered now in a little knot
to talk of their chances, possibilities and proba-
bilities, to surmise and hope; then parted to
move up and down on their island, and so battle against the benumbing power of the keen
winter air. Thus a weary hour passed, — it
might have been years, so slowly it crept, —
and the gray twilight deepened around them.

"Are you very cold?" the doctor asked,
raising Rachel's chilled fingers for a moment
to his lips, then holding both her hands in his
own. The movement was a passionate caress,
but the words were only considerate and kind.

"We must chafe them into warmth. You must not allow chill and numbness to steal your strength, for it will be needed presently. I think in some way they will try to rescue us at the bridge."

"And if they do not? If they cannot help us there?" she asked.

He did not answer directly; only said slowly, after a moment's pause, —

"If all hope fail, when we are sure there is nothing more, I have something to tell you — Rachel."

She scarcely noticed the name, did not wonder at the repressed emotion of the tone. It was no time for commonplaces; intense feeling belonged to such an hour.

The gray deepened into darkness around them, the stars shone out clear and cold in the far-off sky, and still they drifted helplessly on. The afternoon with its light, its safety and companionship, already seemed ages away, so long this dreadful voyaging appeared. The cold wind swept up the river and chilled them through, and the rattle and crashing of ice around them, with the movement of the water, threatened constantly the destruction of their frail craft; and every jar and sound was marked as, with straining eyes, and hearing sharpened to painful intentness, they watched and listened.

They were not left to solitude and darkness. As night fell, fires were kindled here and there along the shore, throwing their red glare out over the water, while their glow along the banks showed many forms moving to and fro. Eager voices hailed them, too — cheering human voices, though wind and ice so often drowned the words. Now and then the lighted windows of some house shone upon them, starlike, from the land as they passed, telling of home comfort, shelter and safety. How common, unthought-of blessings, held so lightly but yesterday, had suddenly grown to inestimable value!

They talked but little as the weary time lengthened, — thought seemed to have passed beyond expression, — only breaking the silence when it grew intolerable. At length, down the river, the bridge began to show dimly, a huge, undefined shape. Then suddenly a light flashed out upon it, another and another followed, until lanterns were swinging everywhere. Eagerly every eye turned in that direction. Kind hearts and strong hands were waiting to help them there, but what would they do? What could they do? Was any salvation possible? Their brittle ice-boat must be crushed to pieces against those massive piers. Every breath became a prayer as they floated onward.

"Look sharp there now! Catch the ropes!" shouted hoarse excited voices as they swept into the shadow of the bridge.

A crash, a jar, the ice swaying and crushing, then stayed for a moment. The doctor's quick hand seized one of the lowered ropes, and his strong arm lifted Rachel forward.

"Quick! place your foot there, your arm through this loop."

"You — ?" she began.

But the prompt imperative tone stopped all parley.

"Be quick! So! Hold fast now!"

It was but a moment. The ice trembled, whirled and crashed upon the pier again, piling its crumbling fragments high around the pitiless stones; but a part broke away, shot under the dark arch of the bridge, and floated out down the river again. It held but two persons.

By the light of the receding lanterns they looked each in the other's face, and slowly realized the danger passed and to come — the hope lost, and the darkened prospect before them.

"Well, comrade," said the doctor's vis-à-vis, drawing a long breath, and trying to speak coolly still, though his voice shook, "we're not dead yet, but our vessel is considerably circumscribed, and we shan't take a long voyage on it, I'm thinking."

From out the gloom and danger, the very shadow of death, Rachel found herself translated at once to light and safety. Sympathizing faces and kindly questions greeted her as she stood bewildered and trembling. Then the throng moved aside for some one to pass; her father's arms enfolded her, and his voice, less steady than usual, exclaimed, —

"My daughter!"

He drew her toward the carriage waiting near; but she awakened to full consciousness with that movement, and swept an anxious glance along the bridge, recognizing the two who had been rescued with her, but looking vainly for another.

"Oh, father! Dr. Kelsey? He saved me."

"Everything shall be done that can be, my dear. There are two still on the ice. But you must go home at once. You are not safe yet, after this terrible exposure."

The carriage robes were piled around her, and she was whirled rapidly away. Her father asked some questions, which she answered mechanically; so, also, she listened while he told her how he had just arrived on the train, and was stepping into the carriage when the tidings met him. Her eyes steadily turned to the windows, watched the swaying lanterns on the bridge as long as they were visible.

In the great house on the hill the girl received a rapturous welcome. But all the warm blankets and soothing potions that faithful Peggy could devise did not for a moment lull her nursling to forgetfulness, until, in the early dawn, came tidings. Far below the town, where the river widened rapidly into the bay, a brave little steam-tug had made its way through the rough waters, and, with great difficulty, rescued the two remaining voyagers, benumbed, almost unconscious, but still living.

CHAPTER IX.

HERBS AND PROPHECIES.

"IT'S an ill wind that blows nowheres," soliloquized Mrs. Shackles, pausing half-way up the hill-road to re-adjust her shawl and change her basket from one hand to the other. "It's dreadful for folks to be carried off on ice, an' such a fuss an' fishin' for 'em! But seein' they *have* been in the cold so long, it's more'n like they'll need a power of boneset or motherwort or some sort of yarb-tea. Leastways they oughter, that's what I say to Humphrey, an' I'm bound to see."

Arriving at the house, it required considerable manœuvring and the employment of skilful tactics to accomplish her object — an interview with the young lady in person. She had a double reason for desiring this. In the first

place, she was more sure of largess from
Rachel's hand, and, besides, she really had a
strong affection for the young girl who had
always humored and been kind to her—
treated her "like folks and not like a poor-
house," as she assured herself. She wanted
to see with her own eyes how she looked, after
her perilous adventure.

That "Peggy Larrison"—her contemptuous
name for the housekeeper—would combat her
purpose, she had a strong suspicion amount-
ing almost to certainty. On the gravelled walk
she paused with a pretence of shifting her basket once more, and surveyed the citadel.
Front blinds closed—no one in that part of
the house then. She followed a winding walk
around to a wing often used as a sitting-room,
furtively scanned it, and then innocently started
as if she had mistaken her way, retraced her
steps, and passed around the house to a sunny
piazza on the south. There a low French window revealed within a cheery open fire, and a

comfortable lounge wheeled before it. A door opened upon the piazza, and Mrs. Shackles' summons sounded there in a moment.

Mistress Larrison answered in person, and scarcely looked overjoyed — a fact that did not disturb the caller.

"Is Miss Rachel here? Land sakes! I mustn't keep the door open a minute for the wind to blow on her," and she pushed in and closed it behind her with marvellous alacrity.

Then she felt safe; and dropping into a chair and drawing off her coarse mittens, she held her hands to the comfortable blaze — scratched, knotted, calloused hands. If they did solicit help, they had also toiled, and life had been hard.

"Sakes, child! I'm glad to see ye safe on that sofy, an' not a-sailin' off on an icicle! Didn't know you was one of 'em till this noon, an' then says I to Humphrey, 'I'll go up. It's like she'll need some boneset now if she's ever a-goin' to.' 'That's right,' says he, 'al'ays take time by the flintlock.' An' says I, ' Humphrey Shackles, time'll be bald-headed afore you ever take it by any kind of a lock.' An' so it will, too — that's why I come. It's dreadful cold, an' I felt powerful weak to-day to walk such a ways, but I thought you might be a-needin' that motherwort."

" No," laughed Rachel, " I am doing nicely without it; but I think we must buy a few bunches, since you were kind enough to bring it."

" Yes, I would child; it's more'n like you'll need it next time," responded Mrs. Shackles, cheerfully resigned to the postponement. " Boneset's 'mazin' good for aches. I'd like to took some myself t'other night, only I hadn't any sugar to put in it, — an' it's 'most killin' without sugar, — so I had to do without, bad as I needed it. An' I hain't got none yet."

" Peggy can give you some to take home with you, perhaps," suggested Rachel with proper gravity.

"Humph! Of course if you wish it, Miss Rachel," answered Mistress Peggy, half provoked, half amused. "Does it take any butter or milk or anything else to make that herb-tea to your taste, Mrs. Shackles? I'm going out to the kitchen now, and I might as well put them all up at once."

"Yes, put up some parcels for her," laughed Rachel, but with kindly glance falling on the gray hair and worn hands.

"'Bliged to ye, child, I jest am!" said the old woman brightening. "Don't know how a body'd get along winters, when there ain't no berries nor nothin', if 'twasn't for neighbors. 'Cause I get to needin' a good many things,— tea and shoes,—an' I won't beg, so I don't have no prospeck of gettin' none unless somebody finds it out accidental like. Wasn't you most froze to death sailin' off that way?" she asked, suddenly changing the subject. "An' that doctor— I 'clare for't doctors is the most curiousest mortals! I s'pose he thought if everybody aboard was goin' to freeze or drown they'd need a doctor along to take care on 'em, though I don't see how he calc'lated he was goin' to be able to do it. But they said the way he le'pt across onto that ice jest when everybody else was skippin' off, it was astonishin'."

"When?" asked Rachel, rousing to sudden interest.

"Why, jest after it broke loose, an' was floatin' off, bless ye! Didn't you see him? They said he come tearin' like a whirlwind down from somewheres near the shore, an' jumped onto that floatin' ice like it was his last chance for life. Like to 'a' been the last thing he ever did do, too, 'cause he was pretty well used up when that steam-tug took him off. Folks asked him what he jumped on for, an' all he'd tell 'em was that he'd expected to jump off again. Now that's that I call bein' dreadful venturesome!"

A rosy flush crept over Rachel's face. She laughed nervously, and tears filled her eyes.

"I think Mrs. Larrison will soon have the packages ready for you — and I am not very strong to-day," she said, abruptly dismissing her visitor.

Mrs. Shackles was quite ready then to accept the implied direction and follow the housekeeper to the kitchen, and once there she was in no haste to depart. Shelter from the cold wind without, a comfortable chair, the pleasant warmth and the tokens of abundance that surrounded her on every side, were all seductive. She arranged with what she considered unusual skill her hints and suggestions of articles that would be acceptable, and when the housekeeper could no longer be induced to understand, she lingered still, basking in the cheeriness of the fire, and bestowing her conversation impartially upon whoever happened to come within range. She discussed the weather, the ice on the river, the late accident, and dropped finally upon an inexhaustible topic — the times.

"Land sakes! but they're hard. Don't look much like it here, but there's plenty of folks that knows it. Bad weather an' lots out of work. An' them that has any is screwed down one month, an' pinched down a little more another month, an' don't get what scantiness is a-comin' to 'em when they'd oughter, so they can't calc'late on nothin'. I s'pose if that young preacher man was 'round he'd think every thing'd go all right, an' they'd get over knowin' they needed vittles an' clo'es if he could preach 'em one of his sermons on the Frinch revolution, or somethin'. There is folks that think they could mend all the rents an' breaks in creation if they jest could get at 'em with their little brush an' bottle of glue.

"Tell 'em to 'conomize! Sakes! why, they can't unless they've got somethin' to 'conomize on. Well, things'll come to a stickin' p'int yet — yes, sooner'n most folks think. Things are a-brewin' an' a-brewin', an' they'll be heard from some day. Some folks'll be 'mazin' 'stonished."

"What do you mean by that?" questioned a rosy-cheeked maid, pausing broom in hand, impressed more by the speaker's emphatic nods than by her words.

"Mean 'zactly what I say," replied Mrs. Shackles, taking care to say nothing exactly, and not quite sure what she did mean, but growing more mysterious on that account. "I don't tell all I hear. There's some things I know, an' more I don't; but every see-saw has got two ends to it, an' when one of 'em comes up the other'll go down. Wait an' you'll see."

The girl stared for a moment in round-eyed wonder, and then hastened away in obedience to a call. But the old woman talked on with or without a listener. She carefully examined her faded dress, and dried by the fire every part that could possibly have acquired dampness from contact with the light snow on the hillside; she warmed her feet slowly and thoroughly, placing but one at a time upon the fender; pinned and unpinned her shawl, arranged and re-arranged the bundles Mrs. Larrison had given her, and lingered until every pretext for tarrying was exhausted, and the lengthened shadows of the great leafless trees warned her of approaching sunset. Even then she went reluctantly, pausing on the threshold with a bright thought.

" Tell Miss Rachel I'll be sure to come round pretty often an' see how she's gettin' on, so if she needs any roots or sassafrax or anything, she can get it handy. I like to be 'bligin', 'specially when folks is sick, if my shoes do be pretty bad to walk so far, an' I can't tell when I'll get no more. I wears sevens."

She wisely closed the door without waiting for reply, and departed with the cheering thought that she would at least be expected again.

Rachel watched her going down the hill as, from her nook among the sofa-pillows, she had watched every one who passed along the road that afternoon. She was not looking for any one, certainly not for the one of whom she was thinking most. The old woman's story had explained his presence with her on the ice, but it had aroused a whirl of thoughts and questions that she could neither still nor answer. She had heard nothing beyond the tidings of his safety in the early morning, but she assured herself that, even with his vigorous strength and power of endurance, it would be days before he could resume his round of duty; yet all the while her gray eyes watched the road.

To see him again his own strong, blithe self, moving once more in an every-day world, would banish that horrible vision of darkness and cold that haunted even yet her closed eyes, she thought. By some strange fascination she found all her reveries continuing that perilous voyage — wondering what would have been had no rescue reached her at the bridge, and she also had been swept through the dangerous arch down the river? What was it he would have said to her when he deemed all hope gone? His words, unpondered at the time, recurred to her now. Again and again she assured herself that it was nothing — her hand but laid upon his lips to restore its vanishing warmth; his words but a deferring all talk of desperate measures until they should find themselves indeed *in extremis.* However she argued it down, the question returned, What would he have said when no hope of life remained?

Old Mrs. Lyndal, insisting that her grandchild should pass the earlier hours of the day in her luxurious invalid room, — the only one in the house, she fancied, where absolute repose could be obtained, — greatly regretted that such shock and exposure had been borne.

"Though all escaped, it is exceedingly unfortunate that it ever happened," she said.

But even she noticed that the girl, with eyes fixed on the glowing coals, did not answer. If she only knew — there might be words worth going down to the gates of death to hear!

But it was nothing. Dr. Kelsey called in a day or two, as usual. Rachel had dreamed, in girlish fashion, of that first meeting — of the way in which she would thank him for the self-forgetfulness, the promptness and courage that had secured her safety, and — should she dare to allude to the way in which he had come to her? But it happened not at all as she had planned. He came, in his accustomed way, to visit Mrs. Lyndal, and Rachel met him in her room.

"I wish you would also bestow some attention upon my granddaughter this morning, Dr. Kelsey, and prescribe proper tonics or restoratives," said the old lady in her stately, deliberate fashion. "It is impossible that Miss Lyndal should not have been greatly shaken and prostrated by her exposure the other night — which only your courage and presence of mind prevented from resulting in a fearful calamity."

The doctor turned and met Rachel's extended hand.

"I do not know how to thank you," she faltered.

"I am glad of it. Pray do not try to learn," he laughed; then added more gravely, "You must not overrate the most natural of acts. In so far as I was of any service to you, the deed was its own full recompense."

He was his cool, quiet, ordinary self, recognizing, apparently, no occasion for gratitude. He inquired after her health in half friendly, half professional style, adverting but slightly to their adventure, and laughing a little at the sensation the papers had made of it. Under his calm manner her glowing grateful thought could find no expression beyond a few brief sentences that sounded to herself exceedingly tame and commonplace.

"We do not forget what we owe you, Dr. Kelsey, but I cannot bear to think of the danger, even yet," said Mrs. Lyndal shudderingly.

"You are right. It is better not to recall it," assented the doctor.

Then the subject dropped. How foolish of her to have thought of anything more! the girl murmured to herself with a causeless flush on her cheeks. Her imagination had grown feverish and wild with the intense excitement of those few hours: that was all. She had not been quite herself, or such insane fancies would never have floated through her brain, she whispered to quiet her womanly pride; and then resolutely strove to forget all troublesome wondering and dreaming in the old avocations that had healthfully busied head and hands. Yet, through the days, when her eyes fell now and then upon those determinedly busy hands, some old words of Mrs. Browning's — meaningless words to her, and she could not tell why they so haunted her — repeated themselves persistently:

> " Kissed
> The fingers of this hand wherewith I write,
> And, ever since, it grew more clean and white,
> Slow to world-greetings, quick with its ' Oh, list ! '
> When angels speak."

When Judge Lyndal first met Dr. Kelsey after that eventful evening he expressed his "sense of great indebtedness" in fitting and proper language, without interruption. Judge Lyndal was not one to be interrupted in any speech he began to make; it must needs have its course. Yet Dr. Kelsey did not find it as oppressive as Rachel's unfinished, stammering sentences had been. He even found a queer thought of addresses before corporations and stockholders flitting through his mind while he listened courteously, and responded as briefly as possible.

In truth, the Judge did feel a weight of obligation that was somewhat burdensome. He disliked debts — personal ones; if it could have been shifted to the company, it would have been a great relief. The chief trouble was that there appeared no immediate way of liquidating this claim. If the doctor had been a man to who he could have offered money, and so settled the matter, or if he had been nearly or remotely connected with the road, so that some lucrative position could have been bestowed upon him, and thus the Judge's appreciation of the service he had rendered be at once handsomely and finally expressed, it would have been an infinite relief. As it was, he could but utter his thanks in words and a clasp of the hand, and wait.

It was only waiting. The Judge had a creed that all benefits were really remunerable; that all services rendered by one man to another would, sooner or later, present their claim for payment in some shape or other. And this would probably prove no exception. Sometime, undoubtedly, some favor or bestowment would be expected of him, without mention, but in remembrance, of this rescue of his daughter; he should grant it, and the obligation would be cancelled. Meanwhile, the impossibility of making any immediate return greatly increased his respect for Dr. Kelsey.

CHAPTER X.

IT was a dreary day, the sky gray with clouds from which fell a heavy mist that never deepened into rain, but had fallen steadily since early morning, penetrating everywhere with its chill and damp, and pressing back upon the little town the black smoke from stacks and chimneys. In the great yard around the shops the general cheerlessness was intensified. Sooty engines stood here and there, some puffing sullenly, others black and lifeless. Trucks, disabled cars, switches, implements, all were chill and slippery with the clinging damp. The great arched doorways of the buildings looked dim and shadowy enough to be the entrances to caverns, while out from the foundry the furnace fires showed only a dull red glare.

Smoke, damp, chill and dreariness over everything, — a heavy oppressive atmosphere that pressed upon spirits, as upon the outer world, shutting out light and hopefulness.

"Never saw anything like this wretched fog," muttered a man in the yard as a wet bar slipped from his grasp.

"Unless it is the company itself — a great, cold, heavy hand, crushing everything under it down, down," answered his companion with lowered voice — a man with keener, more intelligent face.

Joe Baines heard them, but they paid no attention to him — scarcely any one about the place did. All talked before him, seldom any one to him, since he manifested little inclination to join their conversation, and equally small comprehension of their topics.

"A fellow like a crow-bar — good for heavy work, if somebody furnishes the brains to put him to use," one of them said of him; and the verdict was generally accepted.

But Joe felt the gloom of this day. The days in the yard had been growing more and more dreary of late, though he scarcely knew why. He had, in truth, understood but little of the talk of "per cent off," "reduction" and "cutting down" that he heard all around him. The terms so freely used by the others had no very clear meaning for him; but he knew when his wages fell short, again and again, of what he had expected; when all his and Hitty's slow counting, laying out dollar by dollar — pitifully few ! — on the rough table, their two heads bent above it, failed to make the pittance amount to what it had done the month before.

He knew what the falling short meant, too — that the pairs of small stout shoes, so sorely needed, so long promised and looked forward to, could not be purchased; that Hitty's tired, patient fingers must still patch the garments not worth patching, only that no other could be supplied. Such simple, homely little plans of outlay ! but they had meant much in that

old railway-car, and they were thwarted. Joe
wondered silently at first, and then asked a
fellow-workman :

"Why don't I get so much money from 'em
as I did?"

"Why, because there's been a reduction —
ten per cent. Hain't you found that out before?
'Tisn't you, it's all of us."

Joe pondered, not much enlightened.

"Yes; they says something like that to me
at the office. I didn't know. What do they
do it for?" he asked again directly.

"What for? Why, to squeeze a little more
out of our pockets to put into their own, where
there are enough sight more dollars now than
we'll ever have coppers. The treasurer wants
a new steeple to his house, maybe, or the
president a finer palace-car to ride in."

If Joe did not fully understand the language,
and accepted the last sentences literally, he
did comprehend the bitterness of the man's
tone ; that held a meaning that made itself felt,

and, slowly, besides his disappointment, there began to grow and rankle a sense of wrong. So, though he did not know the signs of dull times, or foresee, as did others, any other effects that might follow, the anxiety, dissatisfaction and foreboding around him pressed upon him also in a vague, indefinite way. He wondered, that day, what the two men, talking together, meant by a heavy, crushing hand? Yet, while he wondered, he seemed to feel something of its weight.

But he was utterly unprepared for what came at nightfall — his discharge. There had seemed so much coming and going in the great shops, such an endless amount to do, so much wealth back of it all, that it had never occurred to him that, having once secured a place, he could not stay there so long as he faithfully performed the work assigned him. He looked blankly in the face of the one who told him. It was not a pleasant task, that agent's; he was but obeying orders, he explained. There was no great press of business just now; they were reducing the force of workmen, and some others from the yard and shops would be sent away. Then he grew impatient at the bewildered stare, and cut his communication short by telling him where and when to apply for the money due him.

"I dunno — the folks has to live — I dunno what'll I do," stammered Joe, blundering into speech at last, and drawing his hand across his forehead, as if the mist of the day were creeping over his brain.

"Well, I don't know about that, my man; it's much the same with everybody, I suppose. I'm sorry; but you will have to look about and find what you can do. You've a pair of good strong hands to work with."

There was a touch of contempt in the good-natured pity of the voice. Why not take things like a man? Where was the use of whining?

Good strong hands! Joe looked at them as he walked slowly homeward; looked at them

again in the evening, after he had told Hitty,
and she sat sewing with that anxious unchildlike wrinkle between her brows, and grave
lines about her mouth. He spread out the
broad palms and the great rough fingers.
They were his only capital, his one chance;
all the dependence of his little household — old
Daddy, Hitty and Meg's children.

"Joe," said Hitty, looking wistfully at her
brother's heavy face, "mebby she could get
you in somewheres?"

"The Judge's darter?" Joe slowly shook
his head. "'Tain't no use. They don't want
nobody in any of the places now: they said
so."

He had a vague idea that the fact of Miss
Lyndal's agency in securing the place would
have held it for him if anything could, and
since that had not sufficed, all hope of other
work about the shops was vain.

The next day he wandered through the
little old town, here and there, up and down,

seeking for work. But nobody wanted help — at least his help. He was told so in a variety of ways, civil, careless or gruff, but the import was always the same. The days grew drearily alike — a continual wandering, a monotonous repetition of the one inquiry, and always the same reply. Hitty presently ceased to question when he came home at night to the meagre supper — growing more and more scant as the days passed, for the poor little housewife was economizing their slender store to the utmost. One look at his dull unlighted face told the cheerless story, and she sighed, and stayed her burdened, patient heart on to-morrow — always to-morrow.

It was hard, waiting thus, with that sickening, gnawing anxiety slowly devouring strength and hope, to bestow even the semblance of interest upon Daddy's grand vagaries, that grew only more querulously importunate as the days grew harder.

"Don't ye s'pose it'll come next week, Hitty,

my big prize — how many thousings? Won't
it, child?"

"Mebby, Daddy.

"An' we'll have houses an' new clo'es an'
dinners with meat — we don't have none no
more. Hitty," fretfully, "if you was to tell
them stores 'bout my money a-comin', wouldn't
they let ye have meat?"

"I'm 'fraid not, Daddy; we'd better wait."

Joe extended his search into the country,
going out first in one direction, then in another.
But there was little work to be obtained among
the farmers at that season, and, in truth, the
large, awkward, heavy-faced man, poorly
clothed, and accompanied by his great gaunt
dog, was not a prepossessing applicant. More
than one timid dame fancied the household
would scarcely sleep securely if he were
beneath its roof. This he did not know, but
he soon knew, by painful experience, that
houses or even out-buildings where he could
obtain a place to sleep by honestly asking for

it were very few, so he adopted the alternative of omitting the formality of a permission, and secreting himself when and where he could. One night he crept into a barn, and, beguiled by the unusual luxury of a bed in the hay, and wearied by his journeying, he slept late, and was only aroused in the morning by a rude shake, and a voice demanding in no gentle tones :

"Halloo ! What are you doing here?"

"Sleepin' — I guess." Joe sat up and looked into the irate face of the proprietor as if he were not sure about it. "I had to sleep somewheres."

"Well, I didn't build my barn for a hotel, and I'd like to know how you got into it. Be off now, and don't send any more of your gang here, for I'll warrant you the door will be locked another night. This is no place for tramps."

"If you could anyways tell me where there is a right place for me, I'd be off mighty quick," said Joe, slowly brightening into argument. "For I've looked a long while, an' I hain't found none yet."

It was a very simple observation, but the farmer found it not quite easy to answer.

"Why, there ought to be somewhere, if you are willing to work," he said, somewhat mollified. "More than likely you are not, though."

Joe looked down at his hands. What were they for if not for work? It began to seem as if they had been put into a world where they did not belong. The farmer's eyes followed the mute glance.

"Well, no, they don't look as if they had mostly been kept idle," he admitted as if a question had been asked. "There's my wood-pile over there, and if you've a mind to earn a breakfast by splitting wood, you can have it."

Joe looked at him, looked at the wood-pile, and walked towards it without wasting words. There was no doubt that breakfast was earned. The farmer, watching the heavy steady strokes, raised no question upon that point, and the bountiful meal was such as Joe had seldom tasted. He enjoyed it, too, until a sudden thought made him drop knife and fork.

"What's the matter now?" asked the round-eyed girl who was attending to his wants and keeping guard over the silver spoons.

"Nothin', only Hitty an' the children—an' it kinder chokes," he answered slowly.

The girl's eyes grew rounder still, and she confided to the farmer, a little later, that she "guessed that man was a little out."

"He's sense enough to work, anyhow," responded that practical man, proceeding to suggest a plan that had come into his mind. "Look here," he said to Joe, "I've been intending to have that big shed torn down and moved to the other corner of the lot. I want a new foundation dug, too, and if you choose to stay and help me, why, I'll see what you can do, and pay you what is fair. I don't know how long it will take."

Joe assented eagerly, though with few words. His heart grew lighter as soon as his hands were busy, and he plodded on, obeying directions faithfully, bringing little judgment or skill to the labor, but using his great strength lavishly. Once more he had something to carry to his little household, and his old content gradually returned as the busy days passed. But at the end of two weeks the work was done.

"I like you first-rate, and I'd keep you longer if I had anything more for you to do, but I haven't," the farmer explained. "You see it's rather dull times, too, so a man has to get along with hiring as little help as he can. After two or three months I may need somebody for a while — if you should be along then."

"Yes," Joe answered dully, doubtfully.

And so the dreary wandering began again. Now and then he obtained employment else- . where for a few hours, once or twice for a day or two; but it was only some transient work, nothing that could give steady occupation. These occasional earnings, carried to Hitty, helped to eke out the small sum she so carefully hoarded, but they were only brief respites in his tiresome tramp and quest

Together they traversed the quiet country roads, mile after mile, master and dog — the dog in dumb faithfulness, the master in dumb persistence. Neither knew anything better to do. "Good strong hands to work with!" The words repeated themselves in the stillness of fields and lonely roadsides, and grew into a mockery. He clasped and unclasped the rough fingers, clenched them, wrenched branches from the trees overhead. What was the use of their strength? They were powerless to win bread for Hitty and the children.

In the town he dropped into a way of lingering around the shops and yard, watching the work he could not share. Locomotives, coaches and great buildings, all representing so much wealth, and yet no room for him ! He felt defrauded, wronged, as if this great power of men and machinery were in league against him, crushing him out. He listened eagerly to all the talk he heard about the place, and if he comprehended its technicalities no more clearly than of old, nor followed its reasoning and deductions, he had become alive to complaints and murmurs, and he adopted their spirit, and intensified their bitterness. Somewhere there was cruelty and wrong. Somebody was to blame.

They must live — old Daddy, Hitty and the children. He had promised Meg to take care of the children ; that one thought was clear enough through all. There must be a place somewhere, but he had no money with which to seek it : what they had must be left with Hitty ; and so, penniless and on foot, he started, finally, for a distant city. When he could earn no food by the way, and when he could do no longer without it, he begged it. Sometimes it was

given kindly or carelessly, more than once it
was refused, with the information that a strong
fellow like him ought to go to work. It began
to seem to his dull apprehension that this was
an exceedingly unreasonable world, and that,
somehow, it was at enmity with him.

The city bewildered him. He had never
before been where there was such jostling,
hurrying and crowding as in its business tho-
roughfares. It was not a great city as maps
and statistics of population rated it, but it was
immense in Joe's eyes. It was no place for him;
he realized that fact in a few hours. "Too
many folks here a'ready," he muttered; yet he
tried again and again for work — vainly. He
began to watch the faces and forms of those
who passed him; they all seemed to have
somewhere to go, something to do. He looked
in at the windows of beautiful houses, as he
walked slowly by them — rooms rich with
treasure of which Daddy in his wildest fancies
never dreamed. Why should some have so

much, while others had nothing? The question did not form itself distinctly; it but lay in his thought a sense of injustice and wrong.

At night he wandered back to the only place that had held for him any familiar look — the depot. The trains coming and going, the cars standing here and there, were like the shops and yard at home. Some of them might have come from there — the long iron road connected the two places. He picked his way across rails and around engines, until, at a short distance from the station, he found on a side track an empty freight car, detached, alone and, fortunately, unlocked. As he examined it in the dim light that came from distant lamps, it seemed to him more like a friend than anything else he had met in that dreary, jostling town. He had helped to move such cars often in the yard, in the good times — already they were beginning to seem far away — when he, too, had somewhere to go, and something to do, and could carry home his earnings. Maybe this

car had been there then.   He patted the rough
boards at the thought, almost as if they were
Clingo's rough head.   Poor Clingo! how he
had tried to come with him, and howled and
lamented at being left behind!   It was better to
leave him with Hitty and the children.

"Them little fellers! Wish I could feel their
arms round my neck!"

There was a sudden choking in his throat,
as if the little arms were even then pressing too
closely, as he stretched himself upon his hard
bed.

How long he slept, utterly wearied by the
day's journeying and fruitless search, he did
not know.   A lantern flashing in his face, a
rough grasp and a peremptory voice, aroused
him.

"Here, sir!   Out of that!"

A vigilant member of the police, on his round,
had discovered him.   Any vagrants sleeping
in the cars were a prey to be pounced upon at
once, and he did his duty.   With scarcely

time to open his heavy eyes, Joe was dragged
from his refuge, he did not know why, nor by
whom. His confused, half-uttered protest and
question elicited a brief explanation that but
bewildered him the more. What had "officers"
and "law" to do with him? He had hurt nobody — done no harm.

In his ignorance and alarm he grew belli-
gerent, and thus drew upon his stupid head a
swift blow that in no wise enlightened his fac-
ulties. Then he was hurried again through
the dreary streets, and passed the remainder
of the night in the city prison, with fearful
company. He did not understand much of the
next morning's proceeding, nor know why the
bald-headed gentleman before whom he was
brought should be, as he phrased it, "so down
onto him."

Poor Joe! His appearance was against him.
His blundering, uncommunicative replies, and
the little he told about himself, were unsatisfactory; the way in which he had been found,

and his resistance of the officer, marked him as a suspicious, if not dangerous, character. Moreover, the city had decided to give that pestiferous class — tramps — a wholesome horror of their boundaries; so Joe received a sentence of three days on the city works — a mere salutary warning, it was considered.

The city improved its roads in that way; bands of prisoners, under guard, broke stone to grade its streets and repair its wharves. So there was brief employment found for Joe's strong hands, but no wages to carry home to Hitty. Three days like a criminal on the public works, three nights in that wretched prison den! Joe thought a great deal, for him, in that time. He did not acquire any clearer idea of the law, or the reasons for such treatment; his acquisitions were of another sort, and rapid — bitterness, blind hatred and defiance.

Something was against him, — somebody or everybody, — cruel, tyrannical, unjust, trying to crush the life out of him and his. The antag-

onistic power resolved itself into the one of
which he knew most. The railroad had
cheated him of his wages, little by little, then
it had taken away his work and turned him
out. He could find nothing to do, and was
abused because he did nothing. He had no
money to enable him to travel in search of employment, and was called a tramp, and imprisoned because he travelled on foot and was penniless. He had been dragged out of the empty
car, — the one place where he felt sure of a
right to sleep, — and ill-treated for being found
in it. That, also, must have been the work of
the railroad, he thought; they owned the cars.
Why should they have all the wealth, the right
and power of the world, and crowd him out of
place and bread? Why should this man,
standing guard over him, have the power to
keep him toiling there without wages — the
wages he would have been so glad to earn, at
this work or any other, for Hitty and the
children? He hammered out no answer from

the stones, but the burning sense of wrong strengthened hour by hour.

Once a bright little boy came to the officer's side for a few minutes, was noticed and petted, asked for and received money to spend for some trifle, and trotted merrily away. Joe watched with a sudden fierce gleam in the eyes under the shaggy brows.

"No better'n Meg's babies — no better'n them!" he muttered. "I promised I'd do my level best for 'em, an' now it's this way!"

When the three days were ended he scarcely needed the half-threatening, half-contemptuous injunction to "move on" and not allow himself to be caught there again. He felt no inclination either to linger or revisit the place. Naturally, also, after his experience there, he did not deem it safe to visit other strange cities; so he turned his steps homeward. This time he did not walk quite all the way. He watched the trains carefully, and whenever he could steal a ride of a few miles, he did so. Apart from the rest and help on his journey, he found a satisfaction in doing this. The railroad was his enemy, had wronged him whenever and wherever it could, and anything he could take from it was fair reprisal. Not that he reasoned the subject out thus; he only felt it with a feeling deeper than thought.

He was not shrewd or skilful enough to accomplish his purpose often, or for long, however; and when he did ride unmolested for a few miles, it was more than once because some one, pitying him, chose not to see; but this he did not know. He reached again the little old town, and anxious-faced Hitty welcomed him back, though he brought no good tidings. The twins greeted him rapturously, but, alas! needily, also. The little outstretched arms were not more patient than the wants. Resuming his search in the country, he obtained employment for a few days, and so, once more, added a little to their nearly empty purse; then followed enforced idleness again.

" 'Pears like," said Hitty, dropping her tired hands one night from the little patch she was vainly trying to fit into a large hole, " as if everything was just like that — as if it had to, and couldn't."

CHAPTER XI.

A FAN AND A FACE.

R ACHEL, sitting in her carriage one day, waiting for a few minutes at the station for an incoming train, discovered Joe lounging near.

"Why, Joe! not at work to-day?" she said wonderingly. He seemed to her like a great clock that, once started, would be sure to run on in unvarying monotonous round. Any deviation was unexpected.

"Hain't had none this long time," he answered, something in his voice and manner striking her strangely.

"You have none? How did that happen?"

"Dunno. S'pose somebody wanted my bread-money to buy 'em a few more extrys with," he answered, repeating the thought that, in one form or another, he had heard so often. His eyes fell on the handsome equipage with a sullen look unlike the old satisfied, worshipful glance which he had been wont to bestow upon the lady and all her belongings. She had been kind to him, but she had everything.

Then the Judge came up, and Joe fell back, not unwillingly, and the carriage turned.

"The train is five minutes behind time. We will drive over to the shade of that tree and wait," announced the Judge.

"Oh, father, Joe is out of work!" the girl exclaimed in pained surprise.

"The condition of a good many Joes, my dear," laughed the gentleman. "Whom do you mean?"

"The one who stood by the carriage — Joe Baines."

"Joe Baines?" The Judge reflected a moment. "Oh, that fellow who came to you for a place last summer? Yes, he was sent away some weeks ago, when they were reducing the force of workmen."

" You knew of it, then ? "

" Yes ; I remember now that the yard-master mentioned his name to me about that time, because, I suppose, as I had suggested his coming he thought I might have some special wish for his remaining. Of course I had no preference for one man above another — knew nothing about him, in fact, and had forgotten sending him there. They said he was willing and faithful enough, but an awkward blundering fellow, with a good deal of mere brute strength, and not much wit in the use of it; so he was one of the first to be spared."

Rachel thought of Hitty and of the twins in their wondrous new apparel of which Joe had been so proud. It was strange that she had not heard before, but it was well he had not come to her; she could have done nothing. Only, now that she knew, she would see them.

"Why was the force reduced?" she asked after an interval of silence.

"So many were not needed. Times are rather dull."

"And you could not afford to keep them?"

"Afford?" The Judge laughed. "That is rather an odd way of putting it, my dear. I suspect the company could raise enough to pay their wages — and an inconsiderable trifle besides — if that is what you mean. But really the shops are not carried on for the sole benefit of the men, but in the interest of the company."

She flushed slightly under the good-humored mockery of the tone, but ventured another question :

"The wages have been reduced lately, too?"

"Yes, and salaries of men running on the line. Certainly, the one thing follows the other. When there is an over-supply of labor it commands a lower price, and *vice versa.* Supply and demand regulate the whole matter, Rachel — always have, and always will. But, my dear, you had better leave the subject to business heads. You will find it too knotty to be easily understood."

That was a dismissal of the subject. It was as well, since nothing could be gained by discussing it. The train came panting in, a moment later, and they greeted Nan, for whom they had been waiting. She had only come out for a day or two, the immediate occasion being a party at Craig's Cross. Mr. Corry, having fully and leisurely completed his beautiful house, opened it that night for a grand reception. The cars would bring many guests from the city — a train, indeed, had been placed at their disposal by the treasurer, who liked to do things magnificently upon occasions — and all the arrangements were of a most elaborate and expensive order.

The Judge had knitted his brows for a moment when he first heard what was proposed.

"Rather a pity to do it just now. It is well to pay some regard to popular feeling, even though it is prejudiced and ignorant," he commented. "However, it is Corry's affair, not mine."

Something, it might have been her ignorance of supply and demand, caused Rachel to push aside, almost with a shudder, and lock hastily out of sight some costly jewels when she was dressing that evening. Her cousin rallied her upon the simplicity of her attire.

"Have you lived in this rural atmosphere until you are really metamorphosed into a field daisy? Not but that you look exceedingly pretty," she hastened to add graciously.

Nan was herself in full splendor of plumage and spirits. "I may laugh at Craig's Cross as rural, Rachel, but there is certainly nothing that looks like it in this," she said, as the carriage bore them to the entrance, where a line of carriages was arriving, depositing its gay freight and withdrawing.

"How exceedingly rich and tasteful!" Nan remarked approvingly again as she surveyed

the handsome appointments of the dressing-
room, where the murmur of conversation mingled with the soft rustle of silks and laces, as
gloves were buttoned and flowers and tresses
received a final touch of adjustment. "The
house is almost perfect, Rachel."

She said it as though Rachel, for some reason, might be expected to feel a peculiar interest in this house; but the girl did not notice the
tone, she scarcely heard the words, in a sudden
remembrance of other words spoken long ago.
She wondered if they belonged here?

"Woe to him that increaseth that which is not
his!

"Woe to him that coveteth an evil covetous-
ness to his house, that he may set his nest on
high.

"For the stone shall cry out of the wall, and
the beam out of the timber shall answer it."

They seemed like well-conducted stones and
beams that night, however. If they had any
voices,—moaning, protesting, mournful voices,

—they were drowned by the merry musical ones of the guests, who proclaimed this a brilliant affair. The spacious rooms, with their fair plenishing, their lights, flowers and richly dressed throng, were beautiful as a picture, and Rachel and her cousin found themselves in a moment among a group of city acquaintances who exclaimed and questioned over the choice of the former in spending the preceding winter at home.

"Not that it isn't delightful here, of course, —lovely in summer, — but wasn't it rather dull in winter? It usually is in small towns. Besides, we missed you."

"Oh, was it last winter that you had that adventure on the ice? How romantic!" exclaimed a lady with a waving pink fan which seemed to act as a social bird of prey, fluttering in the atmosphere, pouncing down upon unsuspecting conversational items, and bearing them to its owner for dissection. "Was it just as the papers related it? Do tell us about it!"

Fortunately Mrs. Corry, large-framed and easy-tempered, not over sensitive and a trifle voluble, interposed just there. Though, after her first sentence, Rachel was less grateful for the interruption.

"Oh, you must not try to persuade Miss Lyndal away from home every winter. We are too glad to keep her here, I assure you. Her presence makes the place attractive for certain other people whom business does not leave so free to come and go as you young ladies are," with a meaning glance and smile.

The pink fan darted down upon the suggestion at once, and gave it a little investigating peck.

"Oh! that is it? Now I thought there must be some good reason —"

Then fresh arrivals happily dissolved the group, but later in the evening the fluttering rosy feathers were again at Rachel's side.

"What a charming window-nook this is! Just the place for a cosey chat; and Mr. Stephen

Corry evidently thinks so, for he is coming this way."

If he had thought so,— and it was possible, since the charms of music in an adjoining room had caused the little alcove to be for the time partially deserted,— he was not left to choose upon whom he would bestow his conversation. The bird of prey seized upon his first remark.

"You have been visible at intervals, but you have flitted here and there, like a fair ghost, just out of reach, all the evening," he said to Rachel.

"Which has been half an hour long as yet," she laughed.

"Oh, there is no question that it has seemed longer than that to him!" interposed the fan broadly. "Speaking of ghosts, Mr. Corry, what do you think of these new spirit manifestations — materializations, I mean. Do you know, I attended one of the séances lately? And really it was the strangest thing!"

Nan, talking with a gentleman near them,

suddenly started with half-suppressed ejaculation.

" What is it? " inquired her vis-à-vis and Mr. Corry in the same breath, noticing the movement and her glance of alarm.

" Nothing — a face," she laughed uneasily to cover her momentary loss of self-possession. "It is gone now — a man's face, rough and wild, looking in at that open window. One of the coachmen, perhaps, anxious for a closer view of the pleasures in-doors, but it was so near that it startled me."

"Talk of angels and see their wings," paraphrased pink-feathers briskly. " Perhaps my mentioning the spirits has brought us a manifestation."

" Are you a medium?" inquired a languid gentleman.

" Not consciously. I'm sure I should never choose such a gift, or profession, whichever it is." The talons had clutched another topic with the last sentence, and dragged it forward triumphantly.   "What do you think of women in the professions?"

"Oh, they grace them, undoubtedly," mistily but politely.

"Flattery!   But really I do not see the need for so much talk about 'rights,' 'public opinion,' and all that.   If there is any work a woman wants to do, and can do, why doesn't she stop talking about objections, and insisting that everybody shall be willing, and just prove her right by doing it?"

It appeared probable that the dashing bird would successfully pounce upon, bring to earth and safely dispose of all problems, social, political and religious, before supper.   Mr. Corry, who had gone to order an investigation of the appearance at the window, returned to Rachel.

"Would you like to go to the library?   I have a portfolio of Swiss and German views, some of them very fine, which I should like to show you."

"Annice's judgment will be more valuable than mine." Rachel turned quickly to her cousin. "But we shall both enjoy them, shall we not, Nan?"

"I shall, certainly, but not just now — Mr. Corry will excuse me, I am sure. If Mr. Sheldon will take me to his sister, I must beg to be allowed a little chat with her. I have not seen her since her return, you know."

Her glance and smile said plainly that she considered herself as conferring, gracefully, a favor by her refusal to be included in the invitation. Rachel felt the meshes of the net that was so persistently weaving around her. Why should every one seem so sure of that which had never been defined even in her own thought until it became so as an impossibility? She would gladly have declined to be present that evening if she could have done so, still more gladly would she have refused the *tête-à-tête* that she felt was desired. Her efforts to avoid it had been vain, however; perhaps they had been cowardly also. She arose — there seemed nothing else to do — and with hand just touching his arm walked slowly through the crowded rooms to the library beyond. It was not large, but lofty, and well lined with books and pictures. Folding-doors connected it with the other apartments, and it was in full view of the many promenaders. Still, fewer people were there, and sitting by one of the tables and slowly scanning the views — which Mr. Corry was inclined to treat very unceremoniously when they were fairly before him — there was opportunity for little snatches of quiet talk. He congratulated himself upon this fact after a few minutes.

"For it is a pleasure very rarely accorded me of late. I scarcely ever see you except in a crowd," he added discontentedly. "I saw more of you when you were in the city."

"Yes — you were at leisure, and you were often at my uncle's. — This is Wartburg Castle, is it not?"

"I believe so. Fine, isn't it?" carelessly; then plunging into the other topic again.

"But it is not just that, Miss Rachel. There is a difference beyond mere happening or circumstance — some change in yourself."

He had expected his assertion would be either questioned or explained away, but after a moment she answered simply, —

"Yes, it is true, there is. I have learned more of myself and of my life."

"But should that cause a change towards your friends? towards me?" he asked reproachfully. "We were friends, or I thought we were, and something has come between us. I cannot understand what or why, but I feel it sensibly and painfully."

"No, there is nothing. I think there is no difference that has not always existed," she said slowly and honestly, "only nothing brought it so clearly into view as now. I am older. Life has deeper meanings for me. I cannot take its mere sparkle and foam and be content any longer — that is all."

"And you class me with the froth and foam?"

"No, not that, certainly." She flushed. It was hard to speak the simple truth and yet say no more than it was absolutely needful should be said. "I mean that it was in quest of such things — in our pleasure-seeking that we met so often. We were more frequent companions then, but we are as much — as nearly — friends now as we ever were."

"That is saying very little for any bond between us then," he declared impetuously. "Miss Lyndal — Rachel, I cannot be satisfied to discuss this subject in such a metaphysical roundabout way. It is not simply an interesting problem to me: it is far more. You must have seen my wish, my hope, in all these months, that your friendship might grow to something deeper and stronger — to at least some faint return of the feeling I have cherished for you."

She lifted her earnest eyes steadily to his face for a moment.

"You mistake, Mr. Corry, I am sure you do," she answered gravely, kindly, but with the deliberateness of full conviction. "You are mistaking both yourself and me. It is not really myself that you care for, but only some fancy that you have called by my name. We are too far apart in all our thoughts and plans. We view· everything from a different stand-point. You would see it soon as clearly as I do now."

"Perhaps. I certainly have not viewed this matter in the light that you do — if that is a proof of my moral obtuseness," he said bitterly. Then his pride asserted itself, and he added coldly, "Pardon me ; I have no right, no desire, to press a plea that is utterly distasteful to you."

"I am sorry —" she began. But she could not soften what she had said with any sincere assurance of friendship or esteem, and the broken little sentence had to stand alone.

Through all the talk the sketches had been taken up one by one, held before unseeing eyes, and mechanically laid aside, until half of Germany had been traversed. But now a constrained silence fell that soon grew intolerable. Rachel closed the portfolio at last.

" Shall we return to the drawing-room? " she suggested.

" If you wish ; " and presently they were part of the general stream of conversation and laughter again, with the music floating in ripples and sparkles on the current.

Rachel stole a glance at her companion's face. It was grave, cold and — dissatisfied. An odd little smile crossed her lips as she mentally added that last word. It suddenly reminded her of the Frenchman who expressed his sorrow at the death of his wife by stating that he was " ver mooch dissatisfied." " That is really all in this case," she thought with a sigh of relief. " He is disappointed in his plans, his pride is hurt, but there is no real heart-wound."

The rosy bird of prey swooped down upon them before they had time to separate.

"Have you been looking at pictures in the library? I hear you have some very fine ones there, Mr. Corry. Do you know, I am quite charmed with this place? If I really did believe in women going into professions and business, and all that, I should adopt railroading as my calling at once."

"Not along the line, I trust. It is hard work, — at least it looks so, — and the cabins, though they have the merit of simplicity, are not always constructed upon strictly æsthetic principles."

Mr. Corry might have thought of a dozen pleasanter replies if he had been in an amiable mood, but he was not. The fan fluttered vigorously, and the laugh that sounded above it had a sudden metallic click in it, as if it covered the aiming of a pistol.

"Oh, you think we ladies are so stupid that we should be content with the drudgery? No, indeed, Mr. Corry, I know very well that all the profits are higher up, among the officers. I'd be one of those! There are handsome profits in reducing wages, and not freight or travelling rates, — and in a host of nice shrewd ways that have no drudgery about them. By the way, I heard, the other day, that you and some others — two or three prominent members of your company — had bought a large tract of land out at Henderson. The 'bog farm,' we used to call it: it is so marshy."

" My father and — some others own property there, I believe. Are you interested in transfers of real estate?"

" I certainly shouldn't be in that piece, — it's so drearily flat and malarious, — unless I did belong to a railway company, you know. That might alter the case, for I hear it sold very low, — it surely ought, — and that it will be made very profitable by moving some of the railroad shops out there, and building a lot of cheap houses, which the workmen will either have to buy or rent at the price set upon them. Are the shops to be moved out there, Mr. Corry?"

"There has been talk of removing some of the shops, and that is a favorable point on the line for their location, that is all," admitted Mr. Corry stiffly. "As for the workmen being obliged to go there, that is mere talk, of course."

"But there will have to be workmen in the shops, will there not? and whoever does work there will have to live there, won't they?" persisted pink-fan sweetly.

"They will do so, I presume; they will choose to do so."

"From necessity — yes, I see. Well, I hope their share of the profits will be sufficient to keep them in quinine, for it is a dreadful aguish place, Mr. Corry."

Another whirl of the gay kaleidoscope threw different pieces together, and gave Mr. Corry an opportunity to escape.

"Now, do you know," said pink-feathers turning to Rachel for a parting remark before she whisked away with a blond moustache, "he looked half vexed, but I believe, after all, gentlemen like a lady's conversation to be like wine — with a little *tang* to it."

Rachel answered only with an amused smile, yet under the amusement was a throb of the old pain. Through all the glint and brightness ran the sombre thread of wrong and suffering. A solemn undertone thrilled for her through all the music. And then, with a sudden glance towards the window, she saw and recognized what Nan had seen earlier in the evening, — a haggard face looking in, — a face like that of Joe Baines.

CHAPTER XII.

A WOMAN'S IMPULSE.

THE air about Craig's Cross was heavy with rumors, and the hush of the midsummer day seemed but the stillness of expectancy. Wild stories had flitted over the telegraph wires, and were retold in printed sheets, of uprisings, riots, madness and violence. Like some fierce conflagration, the trouble spread from point to point — for suffering, injustice, ignorance and bitter discontent had been slowly preparing the way, and it needed but a breath to fan the hidden fires to a flame.

The sympathies of the old town by the river were divided. Many condemning lawlessness and violence, yet openly sided with the strikers in their demands, while others reiterated business-like statements of the regulating power of supply and demand. Corporations and individuals had a right to obtain labor at the lowest rates possible, and if the men were dissatisfied, they could seek better places elsewhere. But all the talk of outsiders availed little ; it settled nothing.

" There will be no trouble here," asserted the railway officers with a somewhat nervous show of confidence. "No danger," repeated the authorities of the town. Yet many anxious glances were cast towards the great shops, deserted by their workmen, and, for the most part, closed and silent, while, gathered in groups in the yard, along the line or at street corners, men talked in lowered tones, but with excited faces and eager gestures. There had been no outbreak, but the intense feeling was evident and ominous.

A train bearing several companies of infantry passed over the road, running very slowly through the town, and pausing for a few minutes at the station, so that a full display of the

military force on board was effected. Whatever was the intention of the exhibition, the
result was not desirable. It was regarded as
a menace on one side, and called forth sneer-
ing and wrathful words from the other. Were
the company trying to intimidate them? They
intended to hold their protest against the last
reduction of wages, and were not to be frightened so easily. They had made no threats,
and if the railroad intended that for one, it
would better have been omitted. A resort to
force would not be one-sided.

"There are ways enough, if they have no
more sense than to start that sort of thing.
Trains can be wrecked and shops burned here
as well as at other places. They'd find it
wouldn't pay."

Mere words, wild words, bandied here and
there in the hour's fierce excitement. Those
who uttered them did not for a moment con-
template the deeds of which they spoke. But
there was one lingering now on the outskirts

of this group, now of that, and listening to
everything said, to whom all this was more
than talk. Joe said nothing, and the others
paid little more heed to him than to the great
dog at his side. Both were to them stupid,
good-natured and inoffensive : that was all.

There was something different from that,
however, looking out of Joe's eyes of late —
the look of a hunted creature turning at bay.
The days had grown only harder in the poor
little home. All his efforts could not save its
inmates from absolute want. He seldom obtained employment, and had found, at best,
but transient bits of work that had barely sufficed to keep them in food ; and he could see
no hope or promise for the future. Dark
thoughts thronged his dull brain in his desperation, and he grew more and more at enmity
with the great, prosperous, hard world that
seemed so mercilessly crowding and crushing
him — with the proud, careless ones, who were
flinging away what would be life to him and his.

There was cruel wrong and injustice somewhere, and it became for him embodied in the
power, wealth and activity of the great railroad,
as, day after day, drawn by habit, he wandered
around the place where he had been so glad to
work. The great shops, the far-reaching
lines, the rushing trains with their throngs of
passengers, and the well-dressed officers, holding place and authority, represented to him all
might and treasure. Yet all chance had been
taken away from him to add a little more to
this wealth already boundless. Hitty and the
children must starve for that! They had told
him here to find work elsewhere, when their
power was everywhere to prevent his doing it.
They were the cause of all his weary wandering, suffering and destitution. They had
everything, while he was imprisoned for sleeping an hour in one of their cars.

The utterances of dissatisfaction and sharp
criticism among the men, he had gathered and
interpreted literally; so, also, he placed his

own construction upon what he heard now. There was such a thing as fighting the giant. Others, wronged too far, were taking vengeance, and working ruin and loss in return. He listened with a fierce exultation born of his desperation and pain. Ah! that was a thing to do! Let them learn what suffering, loss and ruin were, too. His strong hands could help that work if they could find no other, and he pondered the new thought.

To Rachel those days were wellnigh intolerable. The storm, long gathering, seemed bursting now, and the comparative quiet of the little town was, to her apprehensive thought, but the hush before a thunder peal. If there had been only danger and no guilt, if she could have stifled the torturing fear that the luxury of her life was built upon a wrong, that a woeful weight of responsibility for these things might rest upon one very near to her, the rest, whatever came, could have been calmly borne. But the old burden pressed more heavily now, and the tangled questions would not separate into threads of right and wrong, so that she could clearly understand.

A feverish unrest was upon her, she could compose herself to no ordinary occupations. She shunned her grandmother's room, where the old lady gravely hoped the law would lay its hands, not only upon the rioters, but upon all malcontents as well. She shrank equally from hearing the talk among the lower members of the household, where all wild and exaggerated rumors were gathered and repeated. She wandered restlessly through the house, until the stillness of the rooms grew insupportable, the atmosphere heavy with doubt and pain, and she sought relief in escaping from it for a time.

She would visit Hitty, she decided, as she passed through the quaint old garden, bright again with all its summer glory. It was no short ramble she wanted, but a long brisk walk, with some definite object in view. Pos-

sibly she could aid Hitty in some way, — she
did not dream how sorely they needed aid, —
and the walk down the hillside, along a
sloping bank above the railway, and through a
strip of wood to the meadow, suited her. There
was sweetness, rest and a freer air under the
overhanging branches of the great trees. Nature, going steadily on with her varied and
beautiful work, smiling in her perfect peace,
repeated some remembered words: "After all,
however things seem to go, the King never
dies, and 'His kingdom ruleth over all.'"
And the troubled heart, hearing, grew calmer.

Hitty's grave face lightened a little at the
sight of her visitor. Such a thin worn young
face it had grown! its look of serious satisfaction and matronly content quite banished by
the anxious lines between the eyes, and the sad
drawing of the mouth. Rachel noticed it even
before she had accepted the chair of state, — the
one velvet-covered seat of the old car, to which
Hitty invited her, — and wondered at so great a

change. It was difficult to obtain any definite
knowledge of their affairs from the child, for,
never voluble, the brave little housewife con-
fined her few remarks to the weather and the
twins, and said not a word of wants. It would
have required a spirit of coarser fibre than Miss
Lyndal's to have disregarded that quiet unchildlike dignity by any direct questioning.
She only wondered and surmised, until she
chanced to inquire for Joe.

"He don't be at home, ma'am, not since
mornin'."

"Is he at work, then?" asked Rachel in
pleased surprise. Something might have happened. Perhaps her father had done something
for him after all.

"Oh, no, ma'am! there don't hardly ever be
no work for him now," answered Hitty as if
astonished at such ignorance. "'Cause Joe's
looked most everywheres. Don't they be hard
times, ma'am?" she asked as if in sudden relief
at finding some one to whom she could speak

of this topic. "I don't know how they'll come now. Joe says it's a sin and robbery to poor folks, and don't ought to be. And everybody do be sayin' it, that them as has been at it ought to lose things, too, and have 'em burned up and took away. I can't just see the rights of it all." She knitted her brows. "Joe do be that down and mad-like, but he says that's how it'll be for evenness."

She uttered it all simply, not seeming to comprehend the full import of what she was saying, or that it could have any special relation to or interest for her visitor. But Rachel shuddered, and interposed hurriedly:

"That is all wrong; it will help nothing — tell Joe so. And Hitty, do not repeat this to any one else — what you have just said to me."

The grave eyes were lifted in wonder at her earnestness, but Hitty only answered quietly:

"No, ma'am, not if you think it do be best not."

"People might misunderstand," Rachel explained briefly. Then she abruptly changed the subject, and turned to the children, poor little Nip and Tuck, who, in garments woefully patched and many-colored, moving monuments of Hitty's skill, were playing near her. She could devise, while she talked with them, no better plan of aiding the little household, and so, presently, placed money in each small palm.

" A birthday gift," she hastily explained to Hitty, who had informed her that they would " be goin' on four next month."

" I may not know or remember the exact day if I wait, and you will know what to buy for them better than I. Spend it as you think best."

It is doubtful if Hitty had ever before known even a mention of birthday gifts; but she accepted it simply, as she did everything.

"Yes, ma'am, we're 'bliged to you," with a queer little bob of a courtesy as the young lady arose.

The call, short as it was, furnished food for thought so deep that Rachel was walking homeward with unseeing eyes for all around her, until, the wood quite passed, some one scrambling up the bank from the railway suddenly stood in her path.

"Sakes alive! You here, child?" ejaculated Mrs. Shackles, as, with bonnet awry and face flushed and excited, she confronted the girl; "I was lookin' for somebody 'mazin' quick. There's rails tore up right down here, an' some trains do run yet, if things is all at sixes an' sevens. Sakes! why, the first one that comes'll be pitched nobody knows where — into the river, most like!"

"Rails displaced! where?" questioned Rachel, rapidly separating the one grain of information from the mass of comment.

"Where I come from, right down the bank here."   ·

She led the way, and Rachel followed to where, along its shelf on the hillside, — a slop-

ing bank above it, but steep descent below, —
ran the narrow iron road. There was a fearful gap in it now, the rails torn up by some
determined hand that had evidently intended
the work of destruction to be thorough. The
girl's face paled as she looked.

"We must get word to the station." She
paused for an instant. Some one must keep
guard there, meanwhile, lest a train should
come from the opposite direction. Their regular running had been rendered impossible by
the trouble at various points, but there was
still communication between Craig's Cross and
the city, and she could not tell when a train
might appear. She dared not leave Mrs.
Shackles in charge, lest, in case warning were
needed, she might fail to give one that would
be understood. "You must go, I think, and I
will watch here. Be sure you make them
know, and send some one quickly. Oh, I
wish there were some one else to go!"

For the old woman's step, though steady,

had lost the fleetness of youth, and she was weary, too, with miles of rambling among the berry-bushes. As if in answer to the wish, a boy appeared upon the river bank, and Rachel's clear call summoned him. He comprehended at once, gave one startled glance at the riven track, nodded intelligently to her brief direction, and, with an emphatic "Yes, *sir!*" sped away towards the town. Rachel watched him out of sight, then turned her anxious gaze to a curve in the road — the first point at which an incoming train could be seen. A light zephyr-like shawl hung over her arm, a fleecy thing of scarlet and white. It must serve as a signal in case of danger, and her fingers rested upon it nervously. Mrs. Shackles had drawn a long breath of relief at the securing of another messenger, and seated herself upon the bank to rest and wait the outcome of the affair.

"Dear! how things do happen! How'd it 'a' been now, if I hadn't come 'long this way with my berries? Now if Humphrey'd 'a' been here, he might 'a' been some use for once. I says to him he'd better come, seein' as I get so tired, an' fetch the berries. But he says, 'No, I'll stick up to my name,'—cause he's heard somewheres that Humphrey means purtector of home, an' it's made him more shif'less'n ever. An' I says to him, 'You purtects home the same way a scarecrow does a corn-field, Humphrey Shackles, — doin' nothin' but hangin' round an' lookin' ragged.' An' so he does, too! Don't s'pose the company'll give any rickompense for savin' that smash-up; an' if they do, that boy'll get it, an' me a-seein' it first, too, an' a-needin' things so bad. But I don't s'pose nobody'll think to tell 'em?" and she cast a sidelong questioning glance at Rachel.

But the girl did not hear her. She still stood by the road, and her glance had fallen upon something lying on the ground near her, beside the broken track — a rough, cheap pocket-knife. Quietly she placed her foot upon it, covering it from sight, waited until Mrs. Shackles' observation was withdrawn, then picked it up and threw it over the bank, as far down among the tangled weeds and bushes as she could send it. She did not ask herself why she did it — she but obeyed an impulse.

The old woman, fanning herself with a huge leaf she had plucked, was again engrossed by her own eloquence.

"Dear sakes! what times! Everybody ag'in everybody, an' all the world crooked. Soldiers a-shootin' an' rioters a-burnin' an' tearin', that's what it's come to! I've been a-sayin' things would happen, but nobody would b'l'eve it. Thought folks could stand everything. They says, 'Half a loaf is better'n no bread.' Course it is! Any fool knows that. But it's the earnin' a whole loaf an' then seein' somebody else slash off the biggest end of it afore ye git it — that's what grinds!"

Rachel did not know how long she talked.

The voice seemèd to run on monotonously for an interminable time, while she stood there watching for sound or curl of smoke around the curve. At last, in the direction of the station, a black moving body appeared, resolving itself gradually into a party of men, guided by the boy whom she had sent. There was no lack of willing hands to aid in repairing the damage, nor of stern voices to express abhorrence of the deed committed, even among those who had suggested the possibility of such retribution befalling the road. They were sincere in their utter condemnation, too. Wild and exaggerated speech might be only an American citizen's prerogative, but an act like this was inhuman.

Rachel lingered but a moment after the relief arrived. She shrank from all questioning, though, indeed, there was nothing to tell beyond the mere fact of the way in which the mischief was discovered. She had not realized how strong was her excitement, nor how tense it had held her nerves, until she was free and all danger past; then she found her temples throbbing and her step unsteady as she walked again along the winding road. A rattle of carriage-wheels sounded behind her, the vehicle drew nearer, and paused at her side.

"Miss Lyndal!" said a quick, clear voice, and Dr. Kelsey sprang to the ground. "You must ride home."

He did not ask her to do so, but his swift glance at her face said that he read her fatigue and unfitness to walk, and she accepted the authoritative tone as "professional," and yielded; nor was she quite sure, in her secret heart, that she disliked that prompt and decided way of taking her in charge. Only she could not talk to any one then. That also he seemed to understand, and, after the interchange of a few commonplace sentences, quietly left her to her thoughts.

Confused and troubled thoughts they were, that, even when she had reached the silence of her own room, she could not disentangle. What had she learned beyond what every one knew? There was nothing to be done, no information to give. Hitty's words had been but a repetition, doubtless, of the talk Joe had heard in many places, from many careless or angry lips. It pointed to no one in particular. Yet even while the girl so assured herself, a fear, so strong that it was almost knowledge, pressed upon her with the weight of a dread secret.

The long slant rays of sunlight faded from hillside and garden, and twilight settled down upon them and enveloped the town below. Yet, even after the roofs and chimneys of the latter were veiled in the gray and deepening gloom, Rachel's eyes turned constantly thitherward, watching for, apprehending, she knew not what. Suddenly the sharp clang of a bell was heard — the quick, imperative fire-alarm, caught up in a moment, and re-echoed by hoarse voices. From the house on the hill a pillar of smoke was discernible in the direction of the shops. Presently it grew luminous, and then a slender shaft of flame shot upward towards the sky.

Standing by an open window, Rachel watched with a shivering dread of something more than loss, while the blaze widened and brightened, then speedily wavered and grew low and lurid, as if beneath some mighty opposing force, and died in clouds of smoke again. With straining gaze she strove to pierce the enfolding cloud, but she could see nothing more, and, forsaking her unsatisfactory post of observation, she threw a light shawl around her, and passed down the walk to the gate. Over the hills beyond the river the moon was rising, showing as yet but a faint line of light. From the town came a confused murmur, a mingling of sounds breaking the stillness of the summer night. But by and by, separating itself and growing distinct, the listener caught the tread of hurrying feet and distant, excited voices, as of some one running, and others in pursuit.

She drew back a little, within the shadow of the arched gateway, as a dark form appeared, showing but dimly in the faint light, and then a heavy panting breath fell on her ear.

"Joe! Joe Baines!" she said with sure intuition.

"They's hard after me," answered Joe in a husky, breathless whisper, scarcely pausing. "I'm 'most beat out."

"Quick! follow me!"

She turned out of the path into the cover of trees and shrubbery, and so, unobserved, hastened towards the house while he followed unquestioningly. Around to a side entrance, through a quiet, unlighted hall, and up a flight of stairs to a remote unoccupied room, she swiftly led the way.

"Stay here, and be silent. Do not attempt to go until I come again," she said hurriedly.

Then closing the door upon him, she enforced her order by turning the key in the lock.

Lanterns were flashing along the hillside, and voices sounded outside the garden wall as she descended to the hall. The pursuers had lost sight of the fugitive. They had been a little further up the road, and turned again baffled.

"He has dodged in here! Must have come in here!" declared a chorus of excited tones at the gateway, and in a moment the lights were twinkling amid the shrubbery. Two or three, leaders of the party, consulted hastily for a minute, then advanced to the house and were admitted.

What had she done! Why had she done it! Rachel did not pause to answer the doubt and question flashed through her mind. She hesitated a moment, and then, as the only natural thing to be done, entered the room from which the voices issued. Her grandmother was there. The alarm of fire had drawn her from her own apartment to the parlors below, which overlooked the town; and the startled servants were lingering about the doorway while the officers explained their errand.

"Yes'm, he was as good as seen to set the fire. It was the carpenter-shop, and meant to sweep the whole thing, but it was discovered soon enough to stop it before any great damage was done. Some one saw him creeping away with sticks and stuff in his hand. We gave chase, but lost him up hereabouts. He must be round here somewhere."

"No one here would harbor such a wretch for an instant," answered the old lady with stately dignity. "We should certainly aid his capture by any means in our power. Judge Lyndal's position is a sufficient guaranty of that."

"Oh, certainly, madam! certainly," interposed the officer, somewhat abashed. "We only meant he might have slipped in unknown, or have been seen by some one who didn't know what he was," — with a glance towards the servants.

They declared at once that they had seen no suspicious character, no stranger of any sort about the place.

"Do you know who he is?" asked Rachel. She wondered afterwards that she had sufficient presence of mind to frame the question, or command of voice to ask it. But she did ask it quite calmly.

"No, ma'am — miss — queerly enough, we've no idea ; only it was some big fellow. He wasn't seen close by, you know. Most likely he was the same one that tore up the track this afternoon."

"Search the grounds thoroughly, or anywhere about the place that you may think necessary. Our people will afford you any help in their power," said Mrs. Lyndal, again expressing the hope that such villany might be speedily brought to justice.

But Rachel said nothing, though she watched the torches and lanterns scouring the grounds unavailingly, and saw the search guided by some of the servants — to whom the sensation and excitement were not a disagreeable novelty — prosecuted even in the lower halls and some portions of the house where a fugitive might possibly have slipped in unobserved. And silently she watched the discomfited band finally turn away and disappear up the road.

A little later her father came, only for a brief stay, however; he was going out that evening by a special train. There would be no further danger at Craig's Cross, he said, so vigilant a guard would be kept. The mischief already done had been, as nearly as he could learn, but the work of one.

"What would be done with him if — if he were discovered?" asked Rachel doubtfully.

There was a sudden flint-like flash in the Judge's eyes, a cold hard ring to his voice, as he answered quietly, —

"He will be sent to the penitentiary — for the longest term the law can give, if my influence or money will avail anything. I would use both unsparingly to have him made a conspicuous example."

The girl's lips closed again over her secret — pale quivering lips that seemed to herself almost Judas-like as, presently, she raised them for her father's matter-of-course, pre-occupied kiss of good-by.

CHAPTER XIII.

AWAY IN THE DAWN.

IN her beautiful room, where every surrounding was a suggestion of luxurious ease and repose, Rachel's light feet paced restlessly that night. To and fro, with bowed head and tightly clasped hands, as if hurrying steps might aid her escape from the maze of conflicting thoughts. What had she done? What must she do? What impulse — was it heavenly or insane? — had prompted her to take into her weak, ignorant girlish hands this fearful weight of responsibility?

At an earlier hour, while some of the household were yet astir, she had borne food to her prisoner; but she had only placed it upon a small table just within the door, and briefly whispered that he must still wait. She could

·decide upon nothing then, and though hours had since passed she still pondered in doubt and dread. Every righteous conviction, every humane feeling within her, shrank in horror from the crimes this man had committed — or attempted. The law laid heavy doom upon such, justly. Had she any right, ought she to have had a wish, to interpose? Was she wiser than all the world besides, that she had dared to thwart its justice and shield this criminal? She knew how sternly nearly every voice would condemn her act; how the most charitable, knowing it, would judge it but the weakest of pity, a short-sighted and culpable pity, that could turn such a man loose upon society again.

Did God view it just the same? she wondered, lifting her eyes. Oh, if she knew! or if the decision could but rest with another! But her own act had made it hers, and she must accept it now with whatever it involved. And more, through all the turmoil of feeling, she could not regret what she had done. Some simple words of Hitty's ran, a steady undertone, through all her perplexity : "I don't know what we'd do 'thout Joe — he do be that good to us. Ever sence Meg died, him an' me has kept us all, somehow." She remembered the unvarying good-nature of his heavy face as she had seen him in the months past, his simple contentment and satisfaction with the hard work that provided so coarsely for his little home; his awkward gratitude to herself, and his uncouth, but honest and unselfish, pride in that burdensome legacy of a dead sister, the twins.

Were others guiltless in this change that desperation had wrought? Did the sin of this day's deed lie indeed no further back than in poor Joe's own dull brain and rough hands? If but a tithe of the money offered so lavishly to procure his conviction and lengthened punishment had been expended in keeping him useful and innocent !

Rachel was no mere sentimentalist. She

cherished no Utopian dreams of having the
world's treasures equally divided. She was
brave enough to have accepted honest poverty
if it had fallen to her lot, and she was cultured
and luxurious enough to have thoroughly enjoyed honest wealth and all it brought. But it
was the knowledge that had come to her
through her share of the road — the wrongs she
knew, and others but dimly surmised — that
made her sometimes feel among these people
almost the humility of one who had defrauded
them. As she looked around her room, rich
and beautiful in all that money could bestow
and perfect taste dispose, a sudden vision of
Joe in prison garments toiling on through
weary hopeless years of bondage — poor, ignorant, desperate, only more brutalized by what
he suffered — smote her with its sharp contrast.

"It shall not be!" she said. "I do not know
if it is Heaven's justice or only a woman's pity
that I am showing, but, at least, God has put

into my hands the power to give him one more chance, and I can do nothing else."

From a small cabinet near her, a dainty combination of pearl and ebony, she drew a roll of bills, smiling half sadly as she remembered the careless lavishness with which they had been given her. "I suppose a marvellous outfit must be arranged for that wonderful reception at Corry's," her father had said, dropping the money in her lap. His paternal duty thus done, he was not one to notice afterwards whether she appeared in velvet or serge ; and for herself she had felt no inclination for display or novelty. So the sum given her had remained intact, and there seemed to her a peculiar fitness in using it as she now designed.

In the gray of the early dawn she sought again the distant room where her captive waited. The dull face — dull still, but haggard and wretched — turned towards her as she entered. . She had not thought what she should say to him, had planned no wise speech of advice or warning, but as she met his look, the words burst forth impetuously :

O Joe ! Why did you do it? "

He began twisting his great hands nervously together, and repeated the thought that had been in his mind for days.

"They've been hard on me — everybody has."

"And you, knowing how hard it is to bear all this, would have brought the same on others if you could? You would burn the shops, and so throw other poor men out of work, and leave their families to suffer as yours has done? " she demanded. "And that broken track — O Joe ! how could you plan so awful a deed? Throwing over that bank cars filled with men, women and little innocent children — those who never harmed you — to be crushed, mangled or burned to death !"

A look of mingled bewilderment and dread crept gradually over his face as he slowly caught the meaning of her words. His eyes opened wide, as if, even before his sluggish sight, a vision of horror were rising.

"I — I didn't think noways 'bout them — the folks. 'Twas the comp'ny," he muttered.

"The company! It would have been only loss of property to them," she said sadly, "only a matter of dollars! But what money could undo all the suffering of those thrown out of work by the burning of the shops, or bring back the murdered to those who loved them?"

Her look and tone seemed to reach his comprehension more clearly than her language. He crouched lower on the floor in the corner where he sat. The uneasy motion of his hands grew more rapid, a visible tremor shook his frame, then he drew a long breath as if trying to shake off some horrible nightmare.

"'Tain't done!"

"No, thank God!"

"So I does." He looked up as if her exclamation had been an injunction. "I didn't mean nothin' to 'em — to them folks. I wouldn't have hurt none of 'em. But it's been hard on me," — going back to the old explanation. "They turns me out, an' I couldn't get no work. They tells me two big hands'll earn me a livin', but they gives me nothin' to do. Went everywheres, an' nobody would have me. If I asks for things to eat, why, they tells me a big beggar like me better go to work — an' I can't get none nowheres. When I goes a-lookin', they locks me up an' calls me a tramp. That's how it's been. 'Tain't no use; there's nothin' — nowheres. Hitty an' the babies must live. I promised Meg I'd take care of 'em, — do my level best, — an' now they're gettin' hungrier an' raggeder —"

There was a choking sound in his throat. He looked down again at the empty, impotent hands.

"I can't do nothin'. There's houses an' houses — I looked in winders, trampin' up an' down — all rich an' soft; an' folks wearin' gold an' shinin' stones, just in their hair or on their

necks, that'd keep Hitty an' the childern.
They has all, an' we has nothin'. 'Tain't right
— God knows 'tain't right ! "

" Aye ! He does ! " the girl answered solemnly, tears standing in the earnest eyes fixed full
upon him.

" An' now it's this way. 'Tain't no use ;
they'll ketch me, I s'pose."

" No," she said, " they will not. O Joe ! I
hardly know if I am right or wrong, — paying
a premium on crime, or saving a soul, — but I
will help you. You must go away. No one
knows who is guilty, but they will if you stay."
For, aside from the hopelessness of his obtaining employment there, she knew that he could
not be trusted to guard his own secret. "You
must leave here and go away to the West.
Far away it is not so crowded, and you may
find something to do ; or you may buy land —
it is very cheap there.

He had been listening attentively, and his
gaze brightened a little as at some new hope.

"If I could anyways — 'cause I helped Meg's husband. It's better'n shops; you can't be turned out."

"Try to get a little place, then, for yourself. You can find where, and this will help you." She placed the roll of bills in his hand. "And as soon as you can, send for Hitty and the children. I will look after them until then."

He looked at her, then at the money in his hand, turning it over slowly. It seemed an immense sum.

"Do not lose it; be careful, and tell no one what has happened here. O Joe —" she paused. As she had once said to Annice Lisle, she was "not good at preaching," but a few earnest words came from her full heart. "Whatever happens, whoever else may be hard, Christ cares. He, too, was poor and ill-treated. For His sake suffer wrong, if you must, but never do it. Some day," dropping unconsciously into an old phrase, "the Judge will come home."

She opened the door, waited while he carefully stowed away the money she had given him, then led the way through the hushed and sleeping house, down to the outer door by which she had admitted him.

" Go over the hill into the country, and follow the highway until you strike the railroad ten or twelve miles from here," she advised.

There was a faint gleam of light across the gray of the east, but the strange, sweet stillness of a summer morning lay over the earth. Until he breathed the outer air, and saw the free road before him, Joe scarcely seemed to understand what had been done for him. He glanced at the sky, then at Rachel, silently, but with a look in his eyes that his dog's might have worn — dumb, appealing, almost adoring. He descended the steps, turned suddenly on the lower one, and pressed his lips to the hem of her white dress, then walked swiftly away.

Languor and heavy eyes awakened neither surprise nor inquiry that morning. The state of affairs in the town, and the alarm of the previous evening, were deemed a sufficient explanation, and Rachel was thankful that she so escaped all questioning; that the fits of abstraction, the pre-occupied manner which all her efforts could not make quite natural, passed unnoticed, or, at least, unremarked. She tried to atone for the night's vigil by sleeping as the morning hours wore away, but slumber would not come at call. She started nervously at every sound. Every step seemed bringing the tidings of Joe's capture; every peal of the door-bell held some message of dread. She was tortured by fears that she had not given him sufficient directions or cautions, that he had not fully understood her, that something she had done, or left undone, would mar all. She was in no mood to review the matter calmly, if indeed there had been use in reviewing it at all.

" Mrs. Lyndal says she would be glad if you could bring your work to her room for an hour or two," announced rosy-cheeked Hannah, pausing at the open door and looking in upon Rachel, whose sole occupation was that of gazing dreamily from the window. "O Miss Rachel, wouldn't it be a dreadful thing if somebody should try to burn this house down? I dreamed about it last night."

"I do not think there is any danger," the young lady answered. Then she thought of Mr. Corry's house and all that had been said of it, and was silent for a moment. "Still I do not believe it will be molested," she said aloud, as the conclusion of her reflection.

"But there's been so many queer doings and troubles," suggested Hannah doubtfully. "And Mrs. Shackles said the other day that there were signs in the sky, too."

"Mrs. Shackles' signs in the sky are like her roots in the earth — a part of her stock in trade," Rachel smiled; and the girl went away, not wholly understanding, but somewhat reassured.

The one topic was everywhere. If she tried to escape from her own tormenting thoughts by talking with any one, it confronted her at the first sentence. She shrank from complying with her grandmother's request, but it could not be refused. Its wording reminded her that she had no employment; and taking up a bit of embroidery, — a mere pretext for busying fingers, — she passed slowly up the stairs, wondering anxiously whether there could be any special reason for the invitation — any information received, or troublesome questions that might be asked. But there was nothing.

"Only this seems the quietest room in the house, my dear, and you must need rest after last night," explained the old lady. "I am not naturally timid, I am sure, but I really was unable to sleep after all the disturbance. The idea of that wretch being secreted somewhere about the grounds, or possibly in the house itself, was horrible! I am sure I should never have thought of it if those men had not suggested it by their absurd search. They seemed so sure that they had traced him so far. You do not suppose it possible, Rachel, that he can be lurking anywhere about the premises?"

"No, I am sure he is not," answered Rachel positively. "I have not the slightest fear of that."

"I did not say that I had fear," said the old lady, slightly resenting that word. "But it would be a very grave misfortune to have such a villain elude justice through any carelessness or over-confidence of ours, aside from any danger of his attempting any further deeds of violence here. I think it might be only a proper precaution to have the servants search the house thoroughly by daylight — every room from attic to cellar, and the grounds and out-buildings."

"Yes; I will go and give the order, grand-mamma," said Rachel hurriedly.

"There is no need, my child; I will ring,"

began Mrs. Lyndal with her usual stately composure. But Rachel arose at once.

"I will explain it to Larrison," she said, and hastened away to avoid further objection, her heart beating quickly with a new fear. What if some trace had been left, some article dropped? She ran to the unfrequented stairway, and followed the route she had taken the previous evening until she stood again in the distant unoccupied room. There was nothing to tell the story. So still, commonplace and undisturbed it looked, that she could have fancied the whole occurrence had been but a feverish dream. Her throbbing pulses grew slower. She went down and conferred with Mrs. Larrison, and returned to the invalid's room again. "I presume they will discover nothing, but at least it will give them something to do, and satisfy them so that they will stop chattering and imagining everything, I hope," commented Mrs. Lyndal, trying to find some good reason for her course other than the nervousness which she was unwilling to confess. "I believe Hannah has been really afraid of every nook and corner she has passed this morning."

"I trust," she remarked presently, "that we shall hear of the miscreant's capture somewhere before the day is over. How perfectly fiendish he must be!"

Rachel's needle traced unevenly a spray of her embroidery, but she was silent.

"But even if he is taken, the law will be entirely too lenient. Imprisonment for such a horrible crime!"

"It was horrible," assented Rachel in a low tone, shuddering as she spoke.

The old lady dropped her hands in her lap — delicate well-preserved hands, despite age and illness — and smoothed the folds of her soft wrapper.

"The penalty ought to include all those who have in any way encouraged or tolerated this movement among the lower classes. The whole uprising is ignorant and suicidal, and shows to what lengths greed and ingratitude will go," she proceeded. "They would ruin their employers and benefactors because they cannot rule everything in their own way."

Through the girl's mind flitted a vague questioning of what foreign element in her own blood, brain or heart had made her see with different eyes from those of her kindred. She glanced about the room with its every appliance of ease and comfort, its costly provision for every hour of pain or languor.

"Grandmamma, did you ever try to imagine how it would seem to be poor?" she asked slowly.

To Mrs. Lyndal this seemed an utterly irrelevant question, and she was not wont to be patient with irrelevancy in any one whom she was honoring with her conversation. Still, if the girl found the subject under discussion too painful and exciting after the events of the previous night, she might be pardoned for seeking to change it. The old lady scrutinized the pale cheeks for a moment, and charitably accepted that conclusion.

"You forget, my child, that I was a Warner before I became a Lyndal — families that had little connection with the very poor, though they did not possess the wealth that my son has since attained," she said proudly. "I certainly have had no experience as one of the class to which you refer, and no cause or desire to imagine myself one of them. In my young days girls were taught to adorn the station in which they found themselves, and not allow their fancies to run wild. What pleasure can there be in imagining one's self in improbable, not to say impossible, situations?"

But, as she watched the bowed head and grave, sweet face, there suddenly flashed upon old Mrs. Lyndal a memory of the child's mother. Her son's marriage with that delicate, sensitive-souled, shrinking girl, whose eyes seemed always looking into a world beyond the every-day one, had always appeared to her the one unwise and incomprehensible act of his life. However, the young mother had died early, and her daughter was as entirely a Lyndal as education could make her.

"Rachel," observed her grandmother suddenly, "I really think that, when these troubles are over, you should go away for a time. The old house is too dull for a young girl like you."

CHAPTER XIV.

AWAY IN THE STORM.

THE long morning, outwardly so beautiful, dragged heavily, but its slow hours passed without bringing tidings of any kind. At noon the bright summer sky clouded. Rachel, in her pre-occupation, did not at first observe it, but when she did, it startled her into action. She must see Hitty that day — must communicate with her herself, and so prevent her making inquiries elsewhere, as she might soon do if she received no explanation of her brother's absence.

She dressed in trembling haste lest a storm might prevent her going, and, though she felt her already overtaxed strength scarcely equal to the walk, set forth on foot, fearing that her carriage might in some way attract attention to the old railway car. Choosing the most unfrequented route, she hastened her steps, but the summer storm swept up swiftly. Clouds gathered and darkened, the thunder changed from low mutterings to louder, more threatening peals, and before she reached the meadow, the rain was falling upon her in heavy, plashing drops.

Hitty met her at the door with an expression of relief.

"I do be glad somebody's come," she said, with a little quiver breaking the usually grave quiet of her lips.

"What is it? Any trouble," questioned Rachel with fast-beating heart. But it was quite different from her thought.

"Daddy. He's been that sick an' queer-like ever since mornin'." She pointed to the cot where the old man lay, pallid and breathing heavily, but with eyes unwontedly bright. "He wasn't just so bad early, an' I thought mebby he'd be gettin' better, so 'twould be only a spell. Then when it be gettin' worse on him, like this, I was feared to leave him to go anywheres. Joe's gone somewheres, he didn't be home all night. There wasn't nobody but me, an' I couldn't leave Daddy 'long of the babies."

Rachel hastily threw off her damp wrappings, and drew a little nearer to the couch.

"You must have a doctor!" she said, shrinking back at the strange look creeping over the withered face.

But even as she spoke the rain fell in blinding sheets that barred, for the time, all possibility of seeking aid. Hitty looked at the driving storm, then back at her visitor silently.

"I will go myself as soon as I can," Rachel answered the glance. "Hitty, I saw Joe this morning. He was going away to find a place and work. I promised to tell you, and look after you. You are to use this, and to let me know when you need anything. He will send for you as soon as he can."

She placed money in her hand — a small

sum, for her treasury was entirely depleted now; but to Hitty, with her frugal ideas of outlay, it appeared no despicable amount.

"I didn't know he did be earnin' so much these days he's out," she said in some wonderment, but with no thought other than that Joe had sent it. "He does often be out lookin' for work, ma'am."

She accepted the explanation so simply and unquestioningly that there was need of saying nothing more, and Rachel sat beside her silently, waiting for the storm to subside. With her transient uneasiness at Joe's absence removed, and a present provision against want, all Hitty's anxiety turned to the old man, her grandfather, lying so helplessly, noticing nothing around him, moaning occasionally, but oftener murmuring brokenly.

"Come to-morrer — houses an' clo'es an' dinners — have dinners, Hitty?"

"Carriages an' velvety sofys an' pianners," answered the child mechanically.

But he did not seem to hear her or to be conscious of her presence.

" Horses, clo'es an' carriages — come to-morrer. Houses an' dinners," he repeated, lingering over the list of treasures that, to his vision, had always been just within grasp. "The prize — to-morrer."

The gray shadow that precluded for him all earthly to-morrows was even then stealing over his face. Rachel, though all unskilled in such reading, could not mistake it. She looked at Hitty questioningly, but could not tell if the grave eyes, watching so steadily, saw as she did. She glanced at the windows ; the storm still forbade all purpose of seeking companionship or assistance. Wilder and more fearful it grew, the wind blowing in terrible gusts that wrenched and tore the trees in its path, and the sky darkening until the narrow apartment lay in twilight gloom except as it was illumined by the glare of the lightning.

Into what strange companionships, what

awful responsibilities, her wandering from beaten paths had brought her, Rachel mused as she sat there. Who, of all who knew her, would dream of finding her in such a place as this? The situation, the darkness and dread of that hour of helpless waiting, was terrible to her already overburdened spirit; but even so she could not wish herself away while this child must bear it all — while the sad dark eyes, looking so large in the pinched, patient little face, turned silently to hers for support and comforting.

Here, at least, there was no talk of the last night's trouble. No rumor of it had reached the old car. With a sudden thought Rachel assured herself of that.

"Hitty, did you see the fire last evening?" she asked.

"No, ma'am," Hitty answered quietly and with no interest.

"Have you seen Mrs. Shackles lately — yesterday?"

"No, ma'am. She don't come these few days."

The old man caught the last words, and moved uneasily.

"Will it come in a few days — a soft bed an' dinners an' everything? Will it, Clary?"

"Yes, Daddy, yes," said Hitty soothingly. "He's called me that by turns all day," she added in a lower tone. "'Twas granny's name, but he's forgot."

"Sing, Clary — sing," quavered the weak voice.

"He do be sayin' that often, too," explained Hitty. "I can't sing nothin', but he do be sayin' it over an' over."

"Sing, Clary — can't ye sing?" The feeble voice broke into a wail.

"If — you could, ma'am" — hesitated Hitty, clasping closely her little rough red hands. "'Cause it do hurt so to hear him."

Something — the little room, the child's face, or some more subtile association — suggested the words heard in the old school-house; and commanding her trembling voice, Rachel sang them again:

> ' For weary feet awaits the street
> All wondrous paved and golden —
> We're going home, we're going home,
> We're going home to-morrow."

They caught the dull ear.

"Home an' goldy streets to-morrer — an' clo'es, Clary — sing!"

In the fury of the storm it seemed as if the world were being torn into fragments around them. Involuntarily to the girl's lips rose that hymn of passionate prayer:

> "While the billows round me roll,
> While the tempest still is high,
> Hide me, oh my Saviour, hide
>   Till the storm of life is past!
> Safe into the haven guide,
>   Oh, receive my soul at last!"

Momently the tempest increased in fury. The lightning came in broad fiery bolts, followed instantly by the thunder in deafening crashes, until it seemed to the excited watchers that earth and sky were but a mingling of awful sound and wrathful flame. The terrified children clung to Hitty and hid their faces in her lap, while she and Rachel sat with pale cheeks. One only was wholly undisturbed by, unconscious of it all. In the brief hushes of wind and thunder came the murmur of his voice, growing slower and fainter.

" Horses an' clo'es for — all on us."

After a time the words varied a little.

" House an' wife an' chil'ren — to-morrer."

Suddenly a gleam of lightning seemed to scorch and blind as if wrapping them in its blaze, while a peal of thunder more terrific than any that had preceded it, shook the old car as if rending it to fragments. Involuntarily they sprang to their feet.

" We do be struck ! " exclaimed Hitty, still holding fast the cowering children.

But a short examination, when they regained sufficient self-possession to make one, revealed the fact that it was not the car, but a great tree close beside it, that had been shattered — riven from its top to the great uptorn roots. It absorbed the attention of all for a few moments, — that evidence of fearful power and of their own narrow escape, — all but that one who noticed nothing. When they turned to him again the feeble voice was stilled, and he lay motionless. The soul had swept out on the tide of the storm. The poor life that had drawn only blanks had passed to seek its possible prize in the "land that is very far off."

Hitty turned to Rachel as if in excuse for her grief.

" He did be that old an' weak an' wandery-like, I know, ma'am, but he was Daddy ! "

The tempest appeared to have spent its strength in that last mighty sweep, and slowly abated. The wind died in long sobbing breaths, the lightning grew less frequent and vivid, the thunder sullen and low. As soon as the rain slackened so that she could venture forth, Rachel threw a shawl around her and left the car. But she paused on the steps. A horse and carriage, detained somewhere by the storm, were speeding along the road that skirted the meadow. She knew the equipage well, the one above all others she would have chosen to see, and her voice — would any other have been heard so surely? — reached its occupant at once.

Her pale face and Hitty's tearful eyes told a story of need that Dr. Kelsey understood more quickly than their trembling words. He made a brief examination of the form lying on the cot. There was nothing for medical skill to do, nothing, indeed, that it could have done earlier, he assured Hitty, who grieved at having been unable to procure it. Then he turned to Rachel, whose questioning eyes were upon him.

"I could not have helped him, but I wish I had been here for the sake of the others — for yours. You must stay here no longer. It has been too hard for you."

Quivering lip and trembling hand confirmed his judgment, though she faintly smiled.

"I did not know I was so weak, but the storm and this—" She left the sentence unfinished. "These children? They must not be left here alone."

"They must not be left here at all," he said in that prompt, decided way of taking the matter into his own hands which was such rest and relief to her. Hitty had told him of her brother's absence in search of work—told it in few words, and as if she had quite understood his going—and that she scarcely expected his return. "There is no need that they should stay; they will be better away, and I will send some one to attend to everything here, and do whatever must be done."

They had drawn a little aside for this consultation, and she glanced at Hitty and the little ones, feeling that Dr. Kelsey could not know the network of circumstances that made it so difficult for her to offer them an asylum.

She asked her next question anxiously:

"But where can they go?"

He had thought of it all, and he answered unhesitatingly, —

"To Mrs. Shackles. That is not far, — just beyond the wood, — and the little girl will want to be near enough to come here occasionally until all is arranged. Mrs. Shackles' home is as good as the place to which they are accustomed, and it is not enough better to trouble or embarrass them. Besides, the old woman will receive them willingly, knowing that she will lose nothing by it, and she will be kind to them. She is an arrant old beggar, but she has one virtue not always possessed by more respectable people — she never preys upon those who are poorer or weaker than herself."

So it was speedily arranged. Hitty yielded quietly to whatever the others thought best. Dr. Kelsey closed the car, and with his carriage packed to its utmost extent — since he was unwilling that either Miss Lyndal or Hitty should remain even while the other was borne to her destination — drove to Mrs. Shackles', and, leaving the children in her care, hastened towards Rachel's home.

Some apprehensive glances he bestowed upon his companion's white face by the way, but he troubled her with few words as she leaned back wearily against the carriage cushions, trying with whirling brain and throbbing temples to lay some plan for the coming weeks.

CHAPTER XV.

WHERE TWO ROADS MEET

THE anxious thought was useless. In the weeks that followed, Rachel could do nothing except to learn, as, sooner or later, we all do, that when our hands are most full, and our work seems to us that which no other can do, even then the world — our own little world — can go on without us.

The events of those perturbed days — the anxiety, fatigue and intense excitement — had taxed her strength too heavily, and wrought their natural result. She struggled bravely against the encroachment of weakness and disease, saying resolutely to herself that she must not, could not, dared not, be ill then. But it was in vain. Nervous chill and burning fever conquered and held sway. It was a slow ex-

hausting fever, no violent illness or delirium —
for that she was inexpressibly thankful, as she
lay a prisoner in her room. A wandering
brain might have proved a woeful traitor.

"Fiddling Simon"—the only name by which
the town had known old Daddy — was quietly
but decently buried by the proper authorities;
and as Hitty simply stated that her brother had
gone to look for work, and that she was to
remain with Mrs. Shackles until he sent for
her, there seemed nothing more for any one to
do, and with that comfortable conviction, few
questions were asked. In truth, unless some
startling disclosure aroused it, suspicion was
very unlikely to fall upon Joe. He was
thought only awkward, stupid and inoffensive
when he was thought of at all, and that was so
seldom that it proved an entire shield now.

With Dr. Kelsey's advice and Mrs. Shackles'
assistance Hitty collected and disposed of her
few effects. Rachel learned of this, and of her
welfare, as she gained nearly all her knowledge

of the outer world in those weary days, from
Dr. Kelsey. To him she entrusted some com-
missions for the child, knowing that he would
accept them quietly, without the explanations
or inquiries she dreaded from others. If he
had felt any surprise at her visiting the car on
that stormy day, or at the deep interest she
manifested in the family, he revealed it by no
question or comment. Sometimes, watching
him, so calm, strong and kind, as he made his
daily call upon her, she was tempted to confide
to him the whole secret. It would have been a
great relief to have shared with him her burden
of solicitude and trouble, to have had the aid of
his clear, manly judgment. But the thought
that the story might prove embarrassing, that a
knowledge of what she had done would make
him, in some measure, a sharer in the responsibility of her deed, withheld her. There
was, too, an added restraint in the consciousness that filial loyalty forbade her explaining
the causes in which her action really had its

root. So, though longing for his aid, she was silent

Once she ventured to ask if the perpetrators of the attempt to destroy the shops and train had been discovered, or any arrests made.

"No, not the faintest clue has been obtained, though for some days they prosecuted the search vigorously," Dr. Kelsey answered. "Interest in the affair is dying a natural death now, and it will probably remain always a mystery."

"No news is good news," runs the proverb, and Rachel comforted herself with it in the absence of anything better. Joe, unheard from, was probably far and safely away. His dull look, and habit of mingling or talking but little with others, might be a safeguard against robbery, and enable him to reach his destination with what he possessed, and expend it as he had purposed, she thought, growing hopeful as time passed.

Weeks elapsed, and the disturbance in the

town and throughout the country had subsided.
Arbitration or compromise had settled the difficulty in some places, in others there was at
least an enforced truce, and business circles
had regained, outwardly, their usual quiet,
before the invalid was able to leave her room.
The day she exchanged her narrower quarters
for a sofa in the pleasant rooms below, her first
visitor was Mrs. Shackles. The old woman,
discovering her, made certain of admittance
by availing herself of the open door without
the formality of knocking.

Amused by her rambling volubility concerning Humphrey, the berries, and the world in
general, Rachel allowed her for a while to talk
at will. But when Dr. Kelsey, whose calls
had become irregular as they became only
semi-professional, came, she dismissed her graciously by bidding her go to Peggy for the
sugar and tea she had intimated " was wantin'
dreadful bad, an' no prospeck."

" But first, how are Hitty and the children ? "

"Oh, they've gone. Sakes! I s'posed you knew 'bout that or I a told it first thing," answered the old woman promptly. "Went day before yisterday — to Oregon, mebby, or Californy. That brother of hers was out there, or cousin mebby 'twas — uncle, or somethin' or nothin'. I don't seem to tell zactly; my membry ain't so good as 'twas." She eyed Rachel furtively as she spoke, trying to discover how much she knew about the children, or whether, possibly, the young lady might not know more of them and their destination than she herself could tell, even if she told all she knew. "Anyway, 'twas somebody as had worked for 'em an' got a place for 'em, an' wanted 'em. An' that girl was chirk as could be to go — no more 'feared than 'sif she'd spent her life a-travellin'. She said Joe wanted her — 'clare 'twas him after all! The letter was so mise'ble mixed up, spellin' an' printin', that 'tain't no wonder I couldn't get it afore. Well, she fixed up them young ones till they looked like a log-cabin bed-quilt, an' they've gone. Wish I had some pieces, an' I'd make a bed-quilt myself," concluded the old woman reflectively. "I could do it between berry spells, an' 'twould be handy to have come winter. But, dear! I hain't got no patches, an' don't s'pose I'll get none."

"I will think of that by and by, when I am stronger," Rachel answered; and, satisfied by what she was sure would be considered a promise, Mrs. Shackles departed.

"Yes," Dr. Kelsey said, meeting Rachel's glance as they were left together, "I came to tell you to-day. Joe sent for them. Accustomed to living as they did here, his preparation for their coming did not require much time. As nearly as I could understand the epistle — it was mixed up, as Mrs. Shackles observed, and far from being easily deciphered — he had possession of a bit of land, and intended to make a home on it. Hitty was able to go very comfortably, and she will carry Joe something besides herself and the twins—though that is considerable, brave little woman that she is! Strangely enough, poor Daddy's last venture did draw a prize. It was no great amount,—fifty dollars,—but it was a fortune to her. When I had secured it for her she looked up at me with her great eyes shining, but she only said, 'Won't Joe be that glad!' She left her thanks for you, and has gone away comfortably and—quietly."

"Oh, I am so glad! so thankful! It frees me from such a burden!" Rachel exclaimed with tearful eyes. Then his last word and something in his look made her add impulsively, "Dr. Kelsey, whatever of all this you know or understand, I am glad to have you know, be sure of that. Do not think I trust you less because I tell you nothing more. The secret is not wholly mine."

"Do you not think I trust you enough to help you without asking why?" he said, betrayed into sudden tenderness by the trembling voice

and the sweet uplifted eyes. "It is more than
trust: I love you. O Rachel, I never meant
to tell you — it seemed unjust to you ! But your
generous feet would not stay in the smooth
bright path to which they were born, you were
always wandering down to the lower and
harder highway where weary and burdened
ones travel. If you will choose this rougher
path, walk it with me — my darling !" for the
fluttering hand slipped into his and rested there.
"Mine?"

"Am I selfish?" he asked again, presently,
as he sat by her side. "Think, Rachel, what
my life must be — not ease and luxury, but constant contact with pain and sorrow. It must
know toil and self-sacrifice, while yours might
be so different. Seeing this, I never meant to
love you, but how could I help it? It is done
for ever and ever —"

"Amen !" added Rachel shyly, with flush
and smile. Then, after a moment: "Why
should you choose nobler, better things for

yourself, and yet consign my life to useless ease without allowing me a choice? Was it such a stretch of charity to think that I too might esteem other things of more worth than purple and fine linen?"

"My darling! My brave, true-hearted little Ray —"

"No," she interposed again, half laughing, but with moistened eyes, "you will find me weak and selfish enough, but you must not begin with the idea that I am to be carried over all the rough places. I will walk with you, and however stony or hard, I want my share of the road."

If he answered with kisses on the bright hair, on the pale cheeks that grew swiftly rosy, and on the little hands he held, the knowledge belongs to her alone — to her only the outpouring of the manly heart's long-repressed tenderness. For Love cannot be photographed, — his glowing face and soulful eyes grow dull and lifeless in the attempt.

The long bright hour drifted by, sunlight and leaf-shadow falling on the carpet, and invisible fingers weaving them into ever changing patterns, while, seated by the sofa, Dr. Kelsey told of his work and his life, his plans and hopes, and Rachel gave in return the sweet new confidence which was yet so perfect that it seemed to have begun ages before. It was her mischievous suggestion that ended, at last, the long talk.

"Have you but one patient to-day, Dr. Kelsey? Your practice is diminishing."

He laughed.

"There is no other case that I have considered so critical. Do you suppose I shall ever know enough, hereafter, to go about my work unless you send me?"

Then, aroused from the pleasant dreaming and planning in which they two only were to be consulted, he remembered to ask the not unnatural question :

"What will your father say to all this?"

"I do not know," she answered slowly, doubtfully at first; then brightening. "But I think you will manage that, Horace, as you do everything else."

He smiled, as he went his way, at the restful confidence of her word and tone, but he was the stronger and happier for it.

"For if she so loves and trusts me, she is surely my very own by a law higher than that of mere place and circumstance," he said. "I was right to tell her — to claim her."

A rightness Rachel never doubted. It did not occur to her — it could not to any woman who truly loved — that there was any sacrifice on her part. His love was her life's crowning, that which dignified it, and made it more sacred and precious than it ever had been before. Whatever Dr. Kelsey might be to the rest of the world, to her he was the embodiment of a wisdom, strength and tenderness in which she rested confidingly, and to which she carried in frank trustfulness, sure that she could not be misunderstood, all her dreams, plans and perplexities — this lonely little Rachel, who had never known mother's, sister's or brother's love.

It astonished Annice Lisle, who, her visit somewhat deferred by the railroad trouble and Rachel's illness, came later than usual. She wondered what her uncle had been thinking of when he permitted such a state of affairs. Bonds and stocks, probably, as usual; and there was no great choice of society at Craig's Cross. But then Rachel could have been elsewhere had she so chosen — and there was Mr. Corry! The whole thing was incomprehensible. Miss Lisle's own delicate hand wore an engagement ring now — a solitaire, valuable but modest, such as was eminently proper for a clergyman's betrothed. She felt, with much self-approval, that she had herself been exceedingly unworldly in deciding her future, though Heman had talent, family, wealth and kindred, desirablenesses of which Rachel had seemed never to think. There must be some renouncing of pomps and vanities; it could not appropriately be a very gay life, that of a clergyman's wife. But how beautiful to give up such things heroically for an exalted purpose! In her cousin's case there could, of course, be no such compensation.

"She may think differently," said Heman, who had arrived for a few days' sojourn, and to whom Nan communicated her wonderings. "A physician's work, you know — well, it might not seem so very dissimilar."

"Heman! The idea of comparing the life of a country doctor, selling pills and curing fevers for *money*, to *your* profession!" exclaimed Annice indignantly.

At which remark, as it floated in to her through an open window, Rachel softly laughed, too blessedly content to care.

CHAPTER XVI.

"TO HAVE AND TO HOLD."

JUDGE LYNDAL was certainly not pleased.
That negative scarcely expresses the state
of his feelings as he paced the length of his
library, measuring his step from heart to heart
of the roses that bloomed in the carpet, while
he pondered Dr. Kelsey's proposal for the hand
of his daughter — a proposal made in a quiet,
matter-of-form way, with no evidence of tre-
pidation, and no mention of her wealth and
his own comparative poverty.

There was something of disappointment in
the Judge's first emotion, though his thoughts
of his daughter's future had never been sufficiently definite to assume the shape of a plan.
He had been conscious of a vague expectation
that she would form an alliance sometime, and

that, of course, it would be worthy of her position and of her father's house. This seemed to him not fully to meet these requirements — in a business point of view, not sufficient return for the amount of capital invested. If Rachel had been a son, ambitious hopes and schemes would have been many, and any thwarting of them keenly felt; but for her he had scarcely been ambitious. The greatest disappointment her life could cause him had been experienced at its beginning — that she was only a daughter. Yet he loved her, after a fashion, and showed it chiefly by allowing her to pursue her own way.

And Rachel could not run railroads nor manage corporations. Whatever alliance she formed, whether she married or not, the name of Lyndal must cease to be a power in the business world when his own busy brain and skilful hands were removed. Nothing would be left of it all except the fortune he had amassed, he reflected somewhat sadly; and that would be Rachel's in any case, and ample though no additions were made to it by any matrimonial contract. The girl might as well have her way, after all. If she were satisfied, the rest did not matter much. She had always an unaccountable fancy for quiet, unostentatious places — and for persons also, he supposed.

Besides, this man had, so far as human judgment could discern, saved her life. But for him he should have had no daughter to bestow. Judge Lyndal smiled rather grimly at this verification of his theory that all favors, however apparently disinterested, sooner or later demand payment. This man set a high price upon his, surely, but it must be paid. Through all his resolving of the subject, the Judge had felt that underlying consciousness — the one conclusion to which he should come. A draft upon him, to whatever extent, must be honored. There was no other manner of liquidating this debt, that had come in this unexpected way, as he had prophesied to himself that it would come in some way, for payment. After all, because of that bit of reflection before mentioned, he became not wholly unwilling.

So he offered his hand to Dr. Kelsey, and with it gave his formal consent. But he could not forbear a single suggestion of the full value — as he understood it — of what he was bestowing.

"Knowing and respecting your character, Dr. Kelsey, there is, happily, no need of my inquiring further into prospects or circumstances. My daughter's fortune will not be insignificant."

If Horace Kelsey winced, it was only inwardly. A smile flashed for an instant under his dark moustache, and vanished in his grave and frank reply:

"I am glad of it, sir — for her sake."

He was far too proud to say, where it would not have been understood, that he loved and sought her for herself alone, and had she been dowerless he would have been even more exultantly glad in his winning—though, in truth, he combated the latter feeling as being less love than pride's subtle selfishness. He attempted not the slightest explanation, only responded heartily when the Judge, who liked to do handsomely whatever he did at all, repeated his acquiescence, more graciously, with expressions of respect and confidence.

If Judge Lyndal considered his daughter's possessions to have been a great attraction, it was not unnatural, and the world would think as the father did. But the doctor's brow, clouding for a little over the reflection, cleared as he rode on his way.

" It may think exactly what it pleases. She is well worth enduring that for, my peerless little Ray ! "

When he recounted to her the important interview, he left that part of it untouched ; but, with the intuition by which she so often answered his thoughts, she said quite irrelevantly of any words he had uttered, —

"There was more, I suppose. Never mind, Horace, we both understand it beyond all mistaking, and it does not matter about others."

No, it did not. He was quite sure of it as he went away from her, with some words from a quaint poem running in his thought:

"Two to the world, for the world's work's sake,
But each unto each, as in God's sight, one."

Neither did Rachel tell him quite all — since there was no need — of a long conversation held in her grandmother's room, when the old lady, after a series of questions, explanations and arguments, became finally convinced that this sole daughter of the house was not formed in the mould of the Warners or Lyndals, and with that conviction ceased to combat the inevitable. After all, her duty done, the outlook had its comfortable aspects for old Mrs. Lyndal. Dr. Kelsey was favored with the close of the discussion in a greeting not unkindly, but sufficiently stately to convey a suggestion of the eminence to which he was to be elevated.

"One favor I must beg, Dr. Kelsey, — insist upon indeed, — that in making your plans you shall not take Rachel permanently away from us. Why should either of you wish it? You cannot find in the town so pleasant a location. The house is amply large, I am growing an old woman now, and, invalid as I am, Rachel will be, as she has been, virtually mistress here. Then, with Judge Lyndal's frequent absences — you really must not think of any other arrangement, at least for some time to come!"

It was not what either of them would have chosen, but in those happy days they were tenderly considerate of all old ties, and the point was yielded for the time. Oddly enough — or it would have seemed so to many of their acquaintances had they talked much of it — among the pleasuring of the bridal tour was planned a quiet, restful visit to the plain old farmhouse among the hills, which Dr. Kelsey had once described, and in this prospect Rachel fairly revelled.

"Do you know, I really wanted to see it that night you described it to Nan?" she said, "though, of course, I didn't think of going in this way. How I did enjoy that evening! It was so queer and delightful."

"A little out of the ordinary boundaries, and you are inclined to be lawless," the doctor declared. "I enjoyed it too — the first of it."

"You grew gloomy and solemn enough at its close, and rode away with a romantically melancholy and majestic air, poor Horace!" she laughed. Then she grew grave again. "I do so want to go to your home as you go to it — not visiting, but *home*," she said wistfully. "Can I really do it, do you think, Horace? Will it seem so to me and to — them?"

"You will like my mother, I know — the dearest, truest mother a man ever had!"

"The first I shall ever have known," interposed Rachel softly.

" And as for her liking my wife — " eye and tone completed the sentence even without the words which were added later, probably upon due reflection : " Bless your brave, tender little heart ! How can she help it? "

In proof of the different opinions that may be held upon the same subject, however, Mr. Stephen Corry, reviewing a little episode in his own history, was at that moment remarking to himself, —

" After all, there are times when it would be exceedingly inconvenient to have an exaggerated conscience for one's household divinity."

Who can tell by what strange ways tidings travel? Some way, the word of this marriage to be, reached a tiny cabin on a far-away plain, where, in her simple housekeeping, Hitty's face had grown round again, and Joe's eyes had regained their good-natured content as he toiled, day after day, upon the little place, concerning which he exultingly assured himself, " It's better'n workin' for folks. Can't be turned off noways; an' ain't them twins a-comin' up hearty?"

There was another question that he often asked himself — "How'd it 'a' been now if she hadn't 'a' done it?" Sometimes in the evening's quiet rest, when the moonlight made a silvery path through the open doorway, and the droning of insects was a chant of peace, or later, when the small room glowed with its cheerful autumn fire, the comfort of it all suggested strange contrasts, and he asked the question of Hitty, "S'pose she just hadn't 'a' done it, how'd it 'a' been now?"

And Hitty, dropping her marvellous needlework in her lap, answered solemnly, —

"Joe, there's things do be worse'n dyin', — that's how!"

This word which reached them caused many consultations, that finally resolved into a definite shape. They wanted to contribute something to the grand occasion, and it must be something magnificent.

" 'Cause common things don't be fit for her,"
said Hitty; " an' common grand things wouldn't
be like nothin', she do have so many."

But something uncommonly grand was discovered nestled among the silk handkerchiefs,
slate-pencils, pins and buttons in the show-case
on the counter of a village store; and when
once the admiring eyes of Joe and Hitty rested
upon it, nothing less was to be thought of.
They planned, worked and saved to purchase
it, and night after night for weeks, with heads
bent together over the table, they slowly scrib-
bled and printed, spelled and blotted, in the
arduous effort of producing an accompanying
epistle.

The result of all this care and labor reached
Rachel, on the morning before her wedding,
in a crumpled, oddly shaped, curiously addressed packet, at which she gazed wonderingly. The document so tediously written was
slowly deciphered also; but, through much
patience, Rachel learned of the humble little

home, its welfare and content; of how the garden had flourished, and of the prospects of the small farm for another year; of the prosperity of Nip and Tuck, and of how Joe meant to do his "level best" for Meg's children. It told, too, awkwardly enough, but with a sincerity beyond question, how they had counted the days in their anxiety that their gift should reach her in time, and how glad and proud they would be to think of her as "a-wearin' of it to be married." And would she sometime let them know if she did?

Because of some allusions, and its suspiciously strong expressions of gratitude, Rachel dropped the missive upon a bed of glowing coals when she had finished its reading; but her eyes smiled with a sweet reverie as she watched it turn to ashes.

"Horror!" exclaimed Miss Lisle, aroused from her usual graceful composure into positive excitement, as she espied among silks, flowers, laces and gems the bracelet that, away on the plain, was considered such a marvel of beauty. "Where did that come from?"

"From Western friends — good friends of mine, though scarcely connoisseurs in precious stones," answered Rachel, with the smile still in her eyes.

But at evening she slipped the trinket on her arm.

"That gaudy, brassy thing, set with a bit of blue glass! Rachel, of what are you thinking? You surely will not wear it?" questioned Annice in astonishment.

The girl looked at it wistfully.

"It will be but for a few minutes; it will harm no one, and it will give so much pleasure — somewhere. See, Nan, this fall of lace nearly hides it."

It did, indeed, like an exquisite frost-work — a delicate tracery of vines and leaves, through which only an occasional gleam of the obnoxious ornament was visible. Annice said no more, but she surveyed again the toilet, perfect to its minutest detail of ornament, clasp and bow, in which she was herself to appear as bridesmaid, and meditated.

"How can she? It is not so much what others would see, as knowing it myself, that would trouble me. It is the sense of fitness through and through that marks the perfect lady. The thought of wearing anything cheap or false at my bridal would be positive pain to me."

But to Rachel that circlet was not so incongruous, and it brought a thrill of grateful gladness as she caught a glint of its doubtful gold through the fineness and beauty above it. It did not make less tender, true or strong the hand she gave that night, and the memory of the words which had accompanied it added depth to many of the more elegant congratulations showered upon her.

All this, however, was but one little episode of the occasion — a slender thread whose weaving in and out was invisible to those who beheld the grand whole. For, notwithstanding the earnest preference of both Rachel and Dr. Kelsey for a more quiet marriage, the Judge had, in great measure, his way. The old house bloomed into a splendor that called forth admiration and some envious sighs, with not a few spoken and mental assertions that Dr. Kelsey was a fortunate man. And he, looking into the clear eyes uplifted to his, called himself more than fortunate, even blessed. But he knew, as no other could, what had been and would be Rachel's share of the road.

Mrs. Shackles, watching the gleaming lights from afar, did not forbid the bans.

" S'pose there'll be less chance to sell 'em motherwort an' boneset, with a doctor in the fam'ly so ; but then there'll be one more to eat the berries. Don't know as I've any objections, Humphrey Shackles."